The Poetry Review

The Poetry Society, 22 Betterton Street, London WC2H 9BX

The Poetry Review

The Poetry Society, 22 Betterton Street, London WC2H 9BX
Tel: +44 (0)20 7420 9883 • Fax: +44 (0)20 7240 4818
Email: poetryreview@poetrysociety.org.uk
www.poetrysociety.org.uk

Editor: Maurice Riordan
Production: Michael Sims

ISBN: 978-1-900771-80-1 ISSN: 0032 2156
Cover illustration Shout / Dutch Uncle

. . .

SUBMISSIONS
For details of our submission guidelines,
please visit the *The Poetry Review* section of
www.poetrysociety.org.uk

ADVERTISING
To advertise, visit poetrysociety.org.uk
or contact Robyn Donaldson on
+44 (0)20 7420 9886,
email: marketing@poetrysociety.org.uk

BOOKSHOP DISTRIBUTION
Central Books, 99 Wallis Road, London
E9 5LN, UK. Tel: 0845 458 9925
or visit www.centralbooks.com

PBS EXCLUSIVE BOOK SUPPLY SERVICE
Readers of *The Poetry Review* can receive many
of the books featured in the magazine post-free
by mail order from the Poetry Book Society.
To order, tel: +44 (0)20 7831 7468,
Mon-Fri, quoting *The Poetry Review*.

SUBSCRIPTIONS & SALES
UK individuals: £34 / Europe: £44
Rest of the World: £49
(all overseas delivery is by airmail)
Single issue: £8.95 plus postage.
Order from www.poetryreview.org.uk or contact
Paul McGrane on +44 (0)20 7420 9881.
Pay by cheque (sterling and US dollar
cheques only), credit card or Direct Debit.

The Poetry Review is also available on audio CD.

The Poetry Review is the magazine of the
Poetry Society and was first published in 1912.
A subscription to *The Poetry Review* is included as
part of membership of the Poetry Society. It is also
available from leading bookshops. Views expressed
in *The Poetry Review* are not necessarily those of
the Poetry Society; those of individual contributors
are not necessarily those of the Editor.

Charity Commission No. 303334

Supported using public funding by
ARTS COUNCIL ENGLAND

CONTENTS

EDITORIAL

"If we are to save poetry," the American poet Richard Howard opined in 1996, "we must restore [it] to that status of seclusion and even secrecy that characterizes only our authentic pleasures." Am I in the wrong job? I've no wish to do poetry damage. But I was hoping to create some diversion by letting so much of it loose in the world. In principle, I can't see any harm in the sharing of pleasure.

At first sight, it seems odd to have such a pronouncement from an American. Ever since the 20-year-old Yeats carried Whitman around in his pocket, poets in these islands have drawn energy, and their newness, from American poetry. It was D.H. Lawrence's joy in *Leaves of Grass* that allowed the breakthrough for *Birds, Beasts and Flowers*, a book which made possible much of Ted Hughes – who in turn enabled Alice Oswald, among others.

And the traffic hasn't been all one way. W.H. Auden in his New York years picked up a few American idioms, and a more relaxed tone – not always appreciated by his English admirers – but he kept to his Old World ways. His example and authority proved decisive for the post-War formalists in America, notably Anthony Hecht, Louis Simpson, Richard Wilbur, the early W.S. Merwin.

Yet this commerce wasn't straightforward. One of the supreme compliments one poet ever gave another was when Auden, on quoting Lawrence's 'She-Goat', noted that the "writing is so transparent that one forgets him entirely and simply sees what he saw". (Try it – and you find he's right.) This urge for plainness, and indeed authenticity transcending the literary, remains an ideal for poets with an American influence. Witness Hugo Williams, interviewed in this issue, taking to task the "Peter Porter style" of poetry for its pretension.

To risk a broad generalisation, those individualistic icon-smashing American poets – the 'Redskins' in Philip Rahv's hoary distinction – have invigorated their British counterparts; while the 'Palefaces' across the Atlantic have looked over here, to Britain and Europe, for the sanction and blessing of tradition. There are of course many complicating unique relationships, such as the one between Frost and Thomas; numerous specific debts as, for instance, Ciaran Carson's to C.K. Williams's long line; the perennial 'discovery' of O'Hara by poets starting out; the almost exclusive devotion of those of my generation to Bishop. It makes for a history of dense and lively interaction.

That the traffic has thinned in the past 25 years is partly due to the scale and compartmentalisation of American poetry nowadays. We find not just many mansions but multiple constituencies, each with its own autonomy, a Switzerland of poetry where every canton, often in practice a university campus, has its own legislature. The overall impression, at least from this distance, is of a blinding snowscape.

It's also the case that, whereas in the 90s poets in this country reconnected with the vernacular, L=A=N=G=U=A=G=E poetry had its brief hegemony in the States. As G.C. Waldrep put it in our Autumn issue, it was not so much that L=A=N=G=U=A=G=E won out, as it "has come to form a key component in American poetry's DNA".

Does this mean the Palefaces have taken over, and the Redskins are in hiding? Well maybe so, for the time being. But it is such polarities that generate the swirl and backlash of energy, the sudden current of experiment and change. We have our own North-South divide, our Roundheads and Cavaliers, Celts and Saxons. It's along such axes poetry thrives.

One specific axis has been that between *Poetry* (Chicago) and *The Poetry Review*. The two magazines started life in 1912, and initially formed a joint force spearheading the modernist revolution. However, Harold Munro, the enterprising editor of this imprint, was soon ousted, and an anti-modernist regime was installed. The two publications have mainly diverged since.

With this issue we risk, along with our new look, giving a new lease to the long-dormant connection by including a selection of poems that appeared last year in *Poetry*. A forthcoming issue of that magazine will carry a reciprocal supplement of work from the *Review*, in what we intend as a regular exchange. Do these American poems sit happily with our own? Well, I'm struck by differences myself: something strenuous in the stretch and flex of the line, giving them a more willed vitality, a noisier heft of the barbells. But I've no difficulty hearing these poems or appreciating their formal strengths – which is as it should be, bearing in mind that it is a poem's ability to make light of the contingencies of cultural difference that enables it to travel, and tests its will to survive.

Maurice Riordan

JAN WAGNER

the castle

after the visits to the sights, the trips across
the country: we balanced on the pin-
nacles of the cliffs, on stones, whose
beards of kelp a midday sun

had begun to dry out,
the barnacles, a fine sizzling,
and retreating into itself the atlantic, pooled between rocks in a few cisterns,

focused upon itself and mute, the capsi-
sed bulk of the beacon buoy
in its frock of rust and that sea-
swallow in the silt,

pungent as a phial of smelling salts: ebb
tide and the entire maritime basement lay
illuminated before us. a crab
sauntered sideways

towards the waves. i was first to spot the prisoner
in one of the brackish eyes:
a great clump of night that ignored
even our sticks and stones, heaving softly

but without fins,
without tentacles or mouth,
flowing into and through itself, a being,
blacker than a power cut,

a bag, swollen with ink, sufficient
even for the longest of all names,
but nameless, and when we returned
it had vanished with the next high tide.

the kings of these estates
hid away in windowless
chambers, peering into the darkness
until they were the darkness, lying in wait

of glad tidings – the word
of one who, entering the hall
confused and blinded by the bright
light of noon, sees nothing at all

except straight in front of him
the tiny patch of sun on the marble floor
that amplifies each step, and the messenger's
time to speak has come.

Translated from German by Eva Bourke.

the burning grove

as if a fragment of the last
evening had snagged on the grass,
as if a flickering shred
of the sunset

were tugging at its thorn: the serene
painting that had been there
earlier seemed to have gone
from the window frame where

we stood, roused by the bell, the donkey heehaws
of the old pump a summons
to join the others in the grove.
instead a chiaroscuro

of bathrobes and tousled locks,
and some near tears.
someone in the pose of laoc-
öon was handling a hose.

the fire grew faster than a shanty
town: a battle for each branch, each
singed trunk, till we staggered silently
around the olive trees,

all of us with the golden fish
of reflection in our water buckets
and an arm held up to the face –
till only shadows were left, blacker

than shadows, the only red
a stripe on the horizon. if not a stroke,
of lightning, what else? an atmospheric
impulse, the flicked-away cigarette butt

of a fire fly? after a while
a cock crowed. a cock. a cock.
and, marvellous as an ocean liner at our backs,
above the hill – the villa,

lit up as for a party whose guests
are still to come, have just left.
how cold it was in our soaked-through clothes
we only felt when the wind rose.

Translated from German by Eva Bourke.

evensong, lago di como

autumn, when chestnuts surrender their weapons,
spiked maces lie scattered on the
ground. in the branches rowan berries
   boast of their

poison. they're all at rest now, the fish hooks
on the bottom, the timber boats in the sheds,
while the leaves transform themselves into smoke,
   the villas take time out

from their splendour, and a border of street lamps
separates the promenade from the lake. the empty
car ferry carries a last cargo of
   light across the water.

Translated from German by Eva Bourke.

GRETA STODDART

Lifeguard

Of course I know he meant nothing to me
alive, why would he, a part-time lifeguard
at the local pool I'd only ever glimpse
slumped in a plastic chair or standing deep
in a cupboard leaning his chin on a mop.
The only thing that ever passed between us
was a look – almost cold from us both –
when I asked him for armbands, the hard kind.
He handed them to me as if I wasn't there.
The day he died I drove past the Tatshack
and saw him outside on the pavement, smoking,
squinting into the late afternoon sun,
his pale dreadlocks flopping down his back,
his bald, stumpy legs. Yes, I remember thinking,
that fits, that crew – pierced, tattooed,
the hair (too much or none), the bikes.
And glancing in the rear view mirror I saw
his big matted head glowing in the dust.
A few hours later I walked into the pool foyer
and there, to one side – a sheaf of lilies
in a mop-bucket and a small table
where a few sweaty carnations were scattered
around a plastic sleeve with three photos:
one of him looking very small on his bike;
another he must've taken himself, it had that
mild looming look of a fish swimming up
to its own vacant reflection; and one of him
hunched over a naked back, needle in hand,
with such a look of care and concentration
I almost felt his breath on the back of my neck.
People were walking past and buying tickets.
Someone was explaining about off-peak times.

It'd been one of those suddenly hot days
at the end of March and there was something high
and reckless in the air. I'd seen a woman
at the lights with huge long breasts in a low black top
and men with their tongues practically hanging out
and I remember thinking here we go again
and the kids in the back were squabbling and my thighs
sticking together and I wanted only to dive into the pool
though I'd never learnt how and wondered now
was it too late and who would I get to teach me?
The road kept on before us, hot and black.
I thought of how big and soft his face was
as if his features hadn't quite finished forming
though already punched with studs and rings and chains
and his eyes seemed swollen and full of something
like he'd cried a lot as a baby or not enough.
He never looked at us. I remember thinking
how could this man save us? How would he know
if one of us just stopped and slipped down
on to the tiled floor? He'd look out across
our bright blue shrieking square
but never at us. Not in the way he is now
like the dead do from their lonely stations
and I'm looking at him in a way I never did
when we lived in the same time, same town
with its narrow streets and muck and diesel air.
Now, when he appears there on the pavement,
smoking and squinting into the light, I see
evermoving water, a slab pinned and still,
a body submerged, a body pierced.
But then, when the lights changed and I pulled away
(let me say this now and without pride) I had you

drugged and disaffected, unfucked and aimless
and I marvelled with some bitterness how someone like you
could ever be sleek and forgetful and strong
in the clear blue streams, could ever have the grace
or urge – however vague – to save a life.
How was I to know I'd just seen a man
in his last light, taking time out for a smoke,
a final look at old Websters' smashed windows,
its drape of red ivy and saggy weeping nests,
an hour or so before he swung a leg
over the new bike, dropped the visor down,
wound his way out in the low evening sun
to the A35, the Little Chef bend, the lorry.

Skull and Hourglass

Hold them there inside that golden room,
their faces flushed, their bellies full of food
and that girl's, surely – look at her smile – with love,
settling its milky pool in some pelvic nook;

hold that man, hale and loud, laughing
down the cleavage of some woman not his wife
whose small black eyes look out at us as if
we might know to keep the secret of her life.

Hold them there before
the old sorrow creeps in
over the bleared plates and sticky rims,
the ruched, exhausted cloth, before the night

has lost all it promised at dusk when the swans
shone their loneliness out on the black lake.

Lamb

The crows were black
coming to and to it
and the dog barking was black
and the trees standing
in a row behind it were black-
trunked black-branched
and a black plastic bag
hung torn inside
the black spaces
and the puddles were black
with mud and ice
and the leaves were black
and the lamb
the crows and the dog
wanted so badly,
the lamb with its
small white splintered
hull of a chest
sticking out so
emptily to the wind
you could almost hear
in the bony tines a tune,
the lamb
was the dead
this early spring
the dead centre of everything

GREGORY LEADBETTER

My Father's Orrery

                        is without end.
The solar system on the fireplace
spins only one planet around its sun –
Mercury, as if now the limit
of what we know, hints at the missing
planets to come, the ache in the equation
their absence makes, the skewed gravity
at work in the hand that hoped to build
a thing of beauty, week by week,
as the advert said, adding to the stock
of wonder. *Just a con, they are.*
Hasn't he got better things to spend
his money on? But I shared the secret
of his joy in those spheres, his maths
by intuition, the theatre of their relative
motion. He showed me the unopened packets,
the grub screws, nuts and pinions of it all,
and there, the planets themselves:
Jupiter, heavy as antique gold,
the ball bearing Earth, Saturn with its halo.
A look of recognition crossed his eyes –
yes, that's them – but out of orbit,
no force to order and bind them
to the weave of their ellipses,
to turn the key of the space between
and spring them in the cradle of their star,
without which, they rattle and fall.
With the planets in his hands, he felt
the weight of his loss, knew he had forgotten
how to put the universe together.

The Fetch

The dream that slammed the bedroom door
but didn't break the film of sleep
to tell the time, or give me more
than broken promises to keep

to phantoms that were never there,
woke me just enough to know
that something was: the restless air,
the waveform of a note too low

to hear, a song to raise the dead.
I listened, and began to speak
as I am speaking now. My breath

condensed. I saw it slowly take
the outline of a child, afraid
of the dark of which it was made.

SARAH WESTCOTT

Messenger

We found her in the shadow
of the gas drum;
a pleat of otherness
pinched from her dominion.

Maw like a whale,
head slit to gill air,
a dark scythe
at our feet.

We willed her wings to open
her form take shape,
conflate to airy spaces.
A new crescent moon.

We picked the whole contraption up,
brindled, tawny, creamy throat;
she spilled over our hands
into awe.

Her claws were shriven,
her eyes the eyes
of something fallen,
the weight unbearable

so we sent her onwards,
to beat at the heels
of a young god's sandals,
set her away, windward.

Form

for Mark Doty

Not snail, exactly –
epithelial
with a tensile foot

like a surfboard
with nerves,
responsive

as any insect
but wet, wet as
reed beds,

sunk root
feeding deeply
in the dark.

Not mussel, exactly,
nor quilled
but a mother, a good mother

of pearl, pressed
with an energy
that sets her edges to fact

each radial spoke
angled in relative
truth

each fold
into a further chamber
enfolding

something of itself.
Here, beneath my finger
like braille,

the clearest patterns
turning and returning
in my palm.

Lambskin

Write me a lambsong,
sing me a skin, yellow curls
coming through, curling to wool,
to warmth, long as a long tongue
licking me –
filling my cells with milk.

We stole the lambskin –
I roll on its song,
we took its song, its young song,
unrolled the curves
laid them over our flat hills.

She places me at the core
where its heart grew –
I am naked in a pool of wool
floating my bones in chambers of air,
lamb wool singing me.

Outside the ewes are calling,
I am the cry and she comes.

MAITREYABANDHU

The Fire Ritual

Take this folded manuscript and write
the names of those who loved you from the start
but mention Jane and how she walked beyond
the runner beans and lettuce to where she'd pick
the damsons while your grandma supervised.

Or after grandma died and Jane stayed on
in that draughty house across the High Street
with the alsatian she fed too many biscuits,
how she'd love to draw the parting in your hair,
dead-straight, with the sharp edge of a comb.

Write about the cushion she'd have to use
to see above the steering wheel and how
she left that day to pick up Mrs Lewis
as usual from the butcher's where she worked,
a taxi job along the Stratford Road.

You knew, when you took the worried phone call –
someone asking where the taxi was,
a policeman in the yard – that nothing bad
could happen if you'd already thought it could.
The news he brought was never talked about.

So write about her here – how cold her hands were
when she woke you up for school! – then burn it
with the naming of her dog, the rug she'd thrash,
peas she'd sit and shell, her stocking-seams,
the soldier she was sweet on in the war.

Birdsong

I don't know which birds
are singing, apart from the pigeon's beat,
   but there's something sweet,
       rapid and short-lived
   at home among the leaves.

I don't know whose trill
this is, this cheerful other song
   further off among
       hedges and tranquil
   wooded lanes – some livelong

anthem Edward Thomas heard
between the whistling shells of France.
   Small recompense –
       a pair of blackbirds
   calling from the distance,

early in black Beaurains.
But I've read the diary he wrote
   standing in his trench coat –
       snow again,
   his boots already soaked,

a photograph of Helen,
continuous bombardment, shrapnel,
   roads that might hide hell
       or lead to heaven –
   lark and partridge, bluebell.

GREG DELANTY

The Sock Mystery

There should be an asylum for single socks,
lost, dejected, turned in on themselves.
The twin sock, soul mate, doppelganger gone AWOL,
on the lam, slipping through a time-space warp
somewhere within the module of the washing machine
or dryer rattling in the cellar's deep space.
The one never to be found again. Gone
we know not where, to the afterlife of socks,
Sock Tartarus; the Elysium of Argyle; the heaven
of crew, gold toe, tennis, winter wooly, tube, summer wear.
Surely there's no purgatory or hell for socks,
even for absconders who walk out on partners, family,
before their soles are worn threadbare, their number up.
The odd time it happens these socks get lonely
for the earth, and weeks, months later the prodigals
meekly reappear under a bed, cushion, wardrobe, only
to discover their partners have disappeared,
passed on, unable to make it alone. But how good
it is to see socks united once more, folded
into each other, close, touching, at one,
the deserter promising to stay put, not to take a hike,
not do a runner this time. No greater joy is known
than on these occasions, such dancing, such cavorting,
such jubilation in the kingdom of socks.

PAUL MULDOON

Colmcille on Exile
from Irish circa 1,000 C.E.

It would be such a blast, O Son of God,
to be able to scud
across the heavy seas
to Ireland, to go back to the exquisite

Plain of Eolarg, back to Benevanagh,
to go back across the Foyle
and listen to the swans
singing at full

tilt as my boat, the Dew-Red,
puts in to port,
with the very seagulls coming out
for a ticker tape parade.

I sigh constantly to be in Ireland,
where I still had some authority,
rather than living among foreigners,
dejected, dog-tired.

A pity, O King of Mysteries,
I was ever forced off my home turf,
a pity I ever got caught up
in the Battle of Cul Dreimhne.

Isn't it well for Cormac of Durrow
to be back there in his cell
listening to the self-same sounds
that once lifted up my soul,

the wind in the elm tree
getting us into the swing,
the blackbird's droll lamentation
as it claps its wings,

the early morning belling
of a herd of big bucks,
the music of summer edging through woodland
from the cuckoos' beaks...

The three things I left behind
I liked best on earth
were Durrow, Derry of the heavenly choirs,
and Gartan, my place of birth.

I so loved being in Ireland
and still rail against being displaced.
To hang with Comgall in Bangor, Canice in Kilkenny,
it would be such a blast.

The Interview

HUGO WILLIAMS

in conversation with Kathryn Maris

O*n my way to Hugo Williams's home in Islington, I recall his 2006 interview for the* Observer: *the journalist opens a paper bag containing cassette tapes, and Williams is affably disappointed to find they are not croissants. I decide to stop at a bakery. When I arrive, late, Williams is waiting for me against his open front door with a forced smile that eases a little when I hand him the croissants. He is lean and dapper in a tweed jacket with a gash from shoulder to wrist. Almost simultaneously, a helmeted messenger joins me at the door with the galleys of* I Knew the Bride, *Williams's new collection with Faber. "It seems awfully short," he exclaims upon opening the envelope, unaware that the galleys are double-sided. Pleased with the cover design, he shows me the mock-up: red letters against a background the colour of Colman's Mustard, the same shade as his hall.*

Like the torn jacket, his little Georgian house, where he has lived since 1966, exudes derelict classiness. Leading me down to his kitchen, he warns me that he and his wife Hermine have just had a "kitchen accident" and that I might smell smoke. After heating the milk for our café au laits, he carries the coffees and croissants on a tray to his study. I'm encouraged to take the armchair while he sits at his desk. The wall behind me is chaotically dense with paintings, prints and photographs; the wall to my left is lined with

Hugo Williams by Eamonn McCabe

(mainly) alphabetised poetry books of which the Ls and Ms are visible from where I'm sitting: Lowell, Mahon, McKendrick, Muldoon. He reflects, "This house was an attempt to make a perfect place to live once upon a time, but now it's got filled up with so many books, it looks like an accident." This reminds me to ask if he went to the celebration of poetry at Buckingham Palace (he did) and if it's true, as I was told by a friend, that the palace is filled with tat reminiscent of Brighton Pier (it isn't). Our interview begins late morning and spans about two hours. We conclude with a fry-up at his local cafe, the Rheidol Rooms, and a walk, with aspects of a guided historical tour, towards Angel station.

KM

You came from an acting family. Your parents, Hugh Williams and Margaret Vyner, are recurring subjects in your poetry. How they met is a fascinating story. Can you tell it?

HW

There's a poem about it in *West End Final*, where my mother speaks about how she met my father. She was a bit of an 'it girl'. She saw him first when he was touring in Australia, when she was about 16. He was unhappily married and hoping to put his marriage together again. She claims to have met him in a nightclub. Anyway she left Australia age 17. She just split, on her own, and came to Europe in 1933. Meeting him was one of her targets. First she had a year-and-a-half in Paris working for Jean Patou as a model, until she was primed for England. But when she came to England, she found it quite hard work. She didn't quite have the manners, I think. She didn't know society. There was quite a lot of prejudice against colonial types, which infuriated her. Once she was in a nightclub when all this fury came to the fore. When she saw a young debutante coming out of the ladies, looking gorgeous, my mother barged into her and knocked her flying against the wall. She told me and my brother this with relish. That's the sort of thing she did, telling stories against herself, being wicked. We were brought up to be bad. We were not brought up with any kind of moral sense at all. Everything was described with vast negativity always, everything except possibly Yehudi Menuhin or Laurence Olivier. The rest of the world was really an extraordinarily unattractive, wicked place, and we were taught to see it that way. My mother and I had this in common – this spitefulness about the world. Mind you, it didn't stop us enjoying it.

KM

Did living in the world, as an adult, change your view of it?

HW

No, I was completely in awe of all that. I accepted all that. That kind of upbringing brought about a critical sense in me that, I noticed, not everyone else has. Not just about books, but about people and about art in general and pretension and all the terrible things in life.

KM

What happened after your mother moved to England?

HW

She started having a bit of success in films and things, and when she heard that Hugh Williams was going to be in a play on Broadway, she got her agent to get her a part in the play, as someone's girlfriend. She and my father were on the same ship to New York. She used to drink milk instead of wine. She was alone at her table, he was alone at his table, and one night he sent her a note saying, "Champagne better than milk, why don't you join me?" When they got to New York, some debonair British actors came down to the port to welcome them in their dinner jackets, and took them both back to a party where the Duchess of Windsor was in attendance. My mother refused to bow or curtsy because she was Australian. She was very proud of that.

KM

Your mother's name appears in the Cole Porter song 'You're the Top' from the musical *Anything Goes*.

HW

Well, I think it was possibly written by P.G. Wodehouse who used to rewrite Cole Porter lyrics for London productions of musicals that Cole Porter had written for a Broadway audience. He would write topical things and she was a famous beauty at the time.

KM

Did you have a sense of your family being special?

HW

It was all over by the time I became aware of it. My father had been through a bankruptcy because of the war and we got a mediocre farmhouse in Sussex, which we paid a little bit of rent for. Life was pretty mundane. Also my father was not very good at keeping up friendships, so there weren't theatrical folk pouring through the house. There were maybe two actors who came round, one of whom was Ian Hunter. That was about it really. The great visitor was my godfather who was the managing director of the Savoy Hotel. He kept us going during the rough times. He came down every weekend in his beautiful car, bearing things from the Savoy. For years we had towels, sheets, everything from the Savoy. And lots of other things: cutlery, cooking equipment, not to mention all the food, wine and things. He'd just bring it all down and we'd take it indoors. He was in love with my mother. He'd been a wartime friend of my father's and my father brought him home one Christmas during the war, and he fell in love with my mother. For some reason my father put up with it, probably because of all the bounty. My sister was almost certainly his daughter.

KM

Did this bohemian childhood, in which you witnessed both bankruptcy and largesse, give you the confidence to fashion a writing life that doesn't include an academic job or the other types of work that poets often have to take on to support themselves?

HW

I never had any respect for work, least of all academic work. I never worried too much about money. I was probably so worried about it that I couldn't bear to contemplate it, so I never did. I never thought about the future. All I ever wanted was to have a bit of peace.

KM

You went to Eton (paid for by your parents' friends, the Astors), a school that would seem to epitomise a certain set of upper class values, including, perhaps, reticence about one's personal life. How are you comfortable being so candid in your poems and prose, given the culture of your education?

HW

Perhaps you learn not to give a damn. "Candour" is something that people pick out in my work, but I can't really see it. It seems to me absolutely essential for writing. Isn't one's life a writer's palette? If you're not going to be candid, you might as well give up. You've got to be candid in order to interest people. I'm very aware of the need to get people reading. For me, poetry is a refined form of entertainment.

KM

What was your life at Eton like?

HW

I'd listen to records and hang out in record shops. Or I'd walk by the river a little bit and try to do some poems. Skimp on my homework. Get somebody else to do it, possibly. Everyone had their own room with a little coal fire. I used to put up pictures: that famous Chinese picture of a horse jumping, and pictures of Brigitte Bardot before she went blonde. And pictures of James Dean. I would sit there and read Laurie Lee or *The Rubaiyat* by Omar Khayyam.

KM

Did anyone encourage your interest in poetry?

HG

I had an older half-sister who was literary and who took me under her wing. She would send me poems. She had made an anthology for my father one Christmas when I was about 12, and she copied all of her favourite poems into this book. He was thrilled with this anthology, which was my first experience of that word, like a strange new science. Not only was it my first introduction to the word, but it was my first introduction to modern poetry, this thing, this anthology, all in her handwriting. So I decided to do one. I got a book and started copying things out. After 12 pages I started running out of poems and making up my own poems to put in. I found it quite easy. You can have a look at it if you like.

KM

You have beautiful handwriting.

HW

Well that was very much part of the aim when I made the anthology. I was trying to copy my father's writing. You could see his character coming through, his incredible, slanted, confident writing. When it was finished, I gave it to him and he was pleased of course. And when he died, I got it back. I found it quite easy to write Laurie Lee's kind of poems, which I thought were mine. That was how I learned to write in a poetic way. I thought Laurie Lee's poems were the way you wrote poems. So I started writing them like that, thinking that was poetry. Of course it's nothing like my voice or my inspiration nowadays, it's just a kind of colourful picturesque writing I was aiming for at the time.

KM

Was there poetry you disliked?

HW

One thing I can't bear in poetry is culture, the subject of culture, as in a certain sort of Modernism. T.S. Eliot could do it. Nobody else can.

KM

How did you feel about Pound?

HW

Pound was *Cathay* for me.

KM

So when you refer to your dislike of "culture" as a subject, you're referring specifically to traits of Modernism as opposed to, say, something more general like ekphrasis, in which a painting is the subject of a poem.

HW

Yes.

KM

You have an ekphrastic poem in your forthcoming collection, *I Knew the Bride*. You were one of several poets commissioned to write about Titian's *Diana and Actaeon*, but you handled the commission idiosyncratically. I suppose you could say you used your autobiographical "palette" for this poem, 'Actaeon', in which all of your ex-girlfriends are gathered in one room.

HW

Yes. The first few lines were written a long, long time before the commission – ages ago – about going into a room and finding all my old girlfriends waiting for me. It's a nightmare I might have, that they're all going to beat me up or something.

KM

So it was a far-fetched revenge scenario?

HW

No, because something like that actually happened to me once. Some girls asked me round. They told me they knew I'd been unfaithful to my girlfriend, who was a friend of theirs. I almost burst into tears with fear and shame. I thought they were going to kill me. And I left. To my eternal shame, I ran away from that confrontation with these girls about their girlfriend I'd been unfaithful to – terrible. And that experience became part of the poem.

KM

You dislike aspects of Modernism, but what about contemporary 'high culture' poetry that is associated with 'difficulty' and/or esoteric references?

HW

It's for the university courses to have something to teach, isn't it? The Peter Porter style of poetry doesn't appeal to me.

KM

Your own poetry tends to be direct, clear and deceptively simple. But any decent poet knows that kind of effortlessness is not easily attained.

HW

It's the dandy or Beau Brummell style of life. It was Beau Brummell who thought that to be well dressed, one's clothes should go unnoticed. It's another version of the Fred Astaire nag: if it looks difficult, you're not working hard enough. Which is maybe a bit corny really. You need a bit of difficulty. This word 'resistance' keeps coming up in academic speech and I don't mind it too much. I quite like the idea of a bit of resistance. It aids memorability.

KM

Are you a perfectionist? Do you tinker with your poems up to the last minute?

HW

I suppose so, yes. It seems to me I just try to improve them.

KM

What are you trying to improve?

HW

I'm trying to get rid of the stupidity.

KM

That's modest.

HW

And I'm trying to get rid of the prose, too. Very often the prose has to get kicked out and maybe possibly put into the title. The title to me is the prose element of the poem. But as for editing: poetry is the only thing I ever made any effort with in my entire life. My poems have been through numerous drafts, numerous, just ridiculous. I keep all the drafts in case I have to go back. I suppose everyone does that

KM

Are your editors heavily involved in this process?

HW

Matthew [Hollis] and Paul [Keegan], my editors at Fabers, were good, picking up bits that were ordinary or cliché-ridden or dull.

KM

Your poetic style is very different to your prose style. Whereas one could describe your poetic style as almost invisible, you are, by contrast, something of a stylist with your prose.

HW

I can't see any difference. If you can't write poetry you can't write prose.

Poetry is the highest thing; it teaches you how to write. I was writing poetry from the age of 13 onwards. I certainly knew how to write sentences from the practice of writing letters home and trying to be interesting.

KM

Many poets seem to approach prose writing with the micromanaging inclinations they apply to their poetry, and they find it a very hard process. Is that your experience?

HW

Well of course it's hard. I find it just as hard to write prose as to write poetry. It's all to do with the struggle to get the sentence right. I see the whole thing as a matter of battling with sentences. Occasionally you find a bit of instruction you can use, like Martin Amis's saying, "Keep the interesting thing for the end of the sentence".

KM

You've said that Robert Lowell's *Life Studies* "was the great breakthrough" for many of your generation, and that it was well into your career that you felt permitted to write about your family and background. When did that sense of permission take hold?

HW

In *Writing Home*. That was when I really loosened up. But I think *Dock Leaves* is my best collection.

KM

Lowell used to talk about "raw" versus "cooked" poetry. He saw his early, formal poems as "cooked" and the poems in *Life Studies* as "raw". Has your work followed a similar trajectory?

HW

That's not quite right. I don't know if I believe in the raw versus the cooked. I think Lowell is being disingenuous about the raw and the cooked, because certainly *Life Studies* is very cooked. Have you ever seen drafts of 'Waking in the Blue'? In one draft, there's a girl who completely disappears by the end of the drafts. I didn't really see it like that: raw versus cooked. I think in order to make this sort of work not seem prosy it has to be really well worked. I should have cooked *Writing Home* much more. I was overexcited about this material, which, rather late in my life, I was getting hold of. And I was thinking, "My God! This is wonderful! All this acting stuff! My father, mother and everything! Who were these people?" Which I'd never touched before. And then my father died. And then, about ten years later, I suddenly got working on it, when I was down in Portugal seeing my mother. But I wish I had "cooked" that collection more.

KM

There's a poem in *Writing Home* that's a favourite at your readings: 'A Collection of Literature'. It that poem really a verbatim letter your prep school headmaster sent your father after discovering a nude magazine under your mattress?

HW

Yes. It was the headmaster's letter to my parents, verbatim, with line breaks put in. It starts, "We have taken from Hugo a collection of literature we found under his mattress". Can you imagine a boy of 12 being asked to see the headmaster, who flips back his blotter to reveal a copy of *Health and Efficiency*?

KM

You must have been mortified.

HW

I nearly shat my pants.

KM

What happened then?

HW

I suppose I was beaten for it. It's a strange thing to be beaten for: taking an interest in the opposite sex.

KM

In 'A Collection of Literature', the line breaks transform the headmaster's letter into a poem. Your line breaks are often distinctive and unexpected. What drives them?

HW

If you say so. It's perfectly beyond description, what makes one break the line. There is one thing I do, which is if I don't want the line to be broken, I break it in an inappropriate place, forcing the reader to go on, as if there were no break. On other occasions, it's an appropriate break and it's something to do with the passage of time. It's where the sadness occurs in a poem. I got that from Ian Hamilton. He understood that, I think. The tears come with the line break.

KM

How important were poets like Ian Hamilton to you and at what point did their influence become less important?

HW

Well, you get these influences and then you try to get rid of them. That's the great thing. And you get rid of them by doing them, by using them, by sort of using them up. I did this with all the early people like Laurie Lee, Thom Gunn, Alan Ross, and then on to Ian Hamilton and Robert Lowell. That would be my list of early influences.

KM

And more recent influences?

HW

Michael Hofmann and Neil Rennie. Neil Rennie taught me a lot. He taught me how French poetry works in English. I didn't get it from Wallace Stevens; I got it from Neil. You assemble your bits and pieces from any given situation but then you don't ask yourself, "What am I going to say here?" but instead you collaborate with the material: you wait and wait, and you try to see what it might give you. Because you're not trying to express something, you're trying to find out something that you didn't know before. That's where the excitement comes. That's where we all get completely obsessed with this subject of poetry, because it seems to make the world become bigger somehow, because you're exploring. So poetry is, to me, research and collaboration. Neil, for example, writes poetry about the South Pacific. For a long time I didn't really get it, and then I sort of understood that this was a way of writing a new world that was strange to oneself. People tend to think you're trying to express something in poetry. I don't think people understand it's a matter of research, collaboration and discovery, finding out something new.

KM

Your poem 'Prayer Before Sleeping' from *I Knew the Bride* seems partly about that process: it's about looking for that first line.

HW

That rather is my method. The thing writes you.

KM

And what did you learn from Michael Hofmann?

HW

Sophistication. He manages to have a tone of voice that's totally his own, that I've never seen in anyone else. He's got a detached, cool tone. That was initially what I fell in love with. I tried so hard to write Hofmann type things, but I never quite managed it. His timing is positively West End.

KM

With your *Collected Poems* you seem to have jettisoned a number of early poems. Was that due to space constraints or did you feel the poems didn't hold up?

HW

I suppose I was thinking of the standards Ian Hamilton set himself and trying to keep to that. And there were jokey poems I didn't fancy much.

KM

Your early poems are quite formal. You favour tercets with an aba rhyme scheme (but not terza rima) and you also use quatrains. Do you remember what drew you to those forms?

HW

Doesn't everybody start out rhyming, because poetry rhymes? But my rhyming never added anything to the cause of a poem.

KM

So it was gratuitous?

HW

It was what Thom Gunn did. My first book was all mimicry; there was no genuine feeling. Ian Hamilton got this absolutely right when he said it's not until the last poem in the book – which I added at the last minute – did I get genuine, real poetry coming through. Everything up until then was mimicry. Mimicry I wasn't even aware of, and which was part Laurie Lee, part Alan Ross and part Thom Gunn. And actually I used to like John Wain, which shows how wayward my tastes were. Even within the Movement poets, I got the wrong one. But I was in love with that tough voice, which seemed an antidote to miserable self-pitying adolescence. It was the Rock 'n' Roll stance you find in Thom Gunn's 'Elvis Presley'.

KM

You've more or less dropped form in recent collections, but one of my favourite poems is your triolet in *West End Final*. Anyone who claims your poems are 'artless' would have to reckon with your formal competence.

HW

I'm not sure my friend Wendy Cope would agree. At some point I tried to write villanelles and I thought I'd invented a new form of villanelle that was unrhymed. But in fact it's not a new form: plenty of people have done it. It's not a bad idea, an unrhymed villanelle: you just keep to the repetition aspect but you don't worry about the rhyme. So I did one. It was made up of two good lines, as usual with villanelles, and the rest of it were just scraps picked up off my desk practically, odd things I hadn't been able to throw away. So I did the villanelle. And it so happened that some of the lines rhymed, as some lines tend to. In fact I think there was slightly more rhyming than usual but it was certainly nothing to do with the prescribed rhyming scheme of the villanelle. So as a joke, I showed this 'villanelle' to Wendy, asking her if I'd got the rhyme scheme right. Almost by return, she sent me a brilliant villanelle whose repeating line was "Not quite, Hugo, not quite," showing me how it should be done. She put that in one of her books, *Family Values*.

KM

Wendy is also a great writer of triolets, funny ones. But your triolet, 'Depression Olympics', has such an odd tone. It seems neither ironic nor unironic. There's often a tonal balancing act in your poems.

HW

It's largely to do with the slowness of the way I work and the untidiness of my desk. The bits and pieces go all over the place and I wait. And 'Depression Olympics' is a perfect example of a poem that is not an expression, but something I discovered. It's also an example of putting the prose element in the title. When I submitted it to Matthew [Hollis] it was called something else. Matthew insisted on calling it that, partly because it was an Olympics year. And it seemed to make sense. I realised maybe it could be about depression, though it's rather poor taste to mention such a subject.

KM

At the risk of poor taste, can I ask if depression has featured in your life?

HW

Am I depressed? Yes, all the time. Especially being ill all the time. Even when I was a boy of 12 I used to get incredibly sad when I was ill. And that has continued. I absolutely can't face being ill at all. I'm fantastically hypochondriacal and constantly take things that are supposed to stop you being ill. Like I always have a little squirter of First Defense in my pocket. [*He squirts it.*] As for depression, once upon a time people dressed in black or purple and went about moaning. It was a wonderful thing. They went into retirement for a period of depression. What do you do for depression? Do you think it's just you, or is it poetry, or your background or some terrible event, or is it just something that you indulge in? I am mystified by it.

KM

I'm mystified too. I suspect there can be an element of all of those things you mention. You've said at readings that you nearly filled up *I Knew the Bride* with dialysis poems, and that writing those poems was a comfort. Has writing always helped to alleviate uncomfortable psychological or physical states?

HW

Writing has always been a natural thing for me to do, the only thing which inspired my energy. With the dialysis poems, I needed them so badly because I was so depressed by this terrible fate. And that's possibly why there might be one or two too many.

KM

I don't think there are too many. It's a wonderful sequence.

HW

I hope you're right. I hope I won't need them to the extent that I'll have to write a lot more. I have actually written another sequence called 'My Next Disease' after a spell of encephalitis caused by being given too much dialysis.

KM

Many of your books are thematic. Those that aren't necessarily thematic often have sequences, such as the dialysis sequence in this new book, or the poems about your mother in *West End Final*, or the daughter poems in *Sugar Daddy*. Do you have a predilection for sequences?

HW

It's all need: to be able to keep writing, sitting at my desk, doing something constructive. That's where it seems to come from. So you've had a bit of fun with this one so perhaps you could give yourself a bit more by trying it from another angle. Also: dissatisfaction with one that's already done. You have another try, perhaps you'll make it perfect this time. Again, it's not really deliberately expressing the whole picture by getting it from different angles. Not at all. It's really just indulging in the pleasure of having material. I mean there are actually other sequences that run across books. There's that one which started off "When I grow up, I want to have a bad leg". That poem generated a lot of spare lines I couldn't use, good stuff that didn't make the final cut, and they got into the next book. And likewise that poem generated more scraps because it's so random anyway. I then started putting the scraps together. In a way that's how I sort of discovered this way of 'collaging' stuff. And there are about six of those poems in the new book, all that came from a poem written 25 years ago, 'When I Grow Up', though the subject obviously changed quite a bit from the subject of the scraps that were left over from the previous ones. I'm sure everyone does that kind of thing. It's not a sequence so much as the simple fact that there are six crazy poems that go back to one poem from 25 years ago. But sequences. That's an interesting question. I've never thought of that before. It seems so cold-blooded, this notion of sequences. People put numbers on them. It sounds so deliberate: "1, 2, 3, 4. Then we broke up and got back together, etc." It's not so much I want to give the whole picture but perhaps, as I was saying earlier, I want to find out more about a subject.

KM

Do you ever exhaust a subject? You seem to come back to the father a lot.

HW

I come back to everything. I only have two subjects. But I've finished with the father now.

KM

Years ago, at a poetry event, we talked at cross purposes for at least 20 minutes. You were talking about John Betjeman, but I heard "John Berryman". Somehow we managed to have a coherent dialogue around this surreal misunderstanding. In retrospect, I should have realised you'd be talking about Betjeman, because you'd recently edited a selection of his poems for Faber. What drew you to him?

HW

That would have been Paul [Keegan], my editor, who suggested John Betjeman. It's the middlebrow aspect of Betjeman that Paul thought I might be able to handle. You don't really have to treat Betjeman in an academic way, which was clearly beyond me, since my education stopped at 17. Most universities were only built in the 60s. Now half the population go to university. That was completely out of the question back then. Even my close friend, Guy Brett, who became the art critic of the *Times*, didn't go to university. He got a job. We all got jobs at the age of 17. I worked in a shop in Piccadilly, Simpson's. It's now become a Waterstones.

KM

Simpson's, the department store? What department were you in?

HW

The mail order department. It was perfect. All I had to do was go around with a big basket, collecting people's orders from the different departments, like the ski department, where I knew someone I could chat with, and then down to the shoe department to get some shoes, and then I'd take it all back to the mail order department. Along the way I could waste hours in the gents halfway up the stairs. I spent half my time reading in that lavatory. This was back in the 1960s, but the lavatory is still there, halfway up the stairs, in Waterstones. I find that one of the fascinating things about London: that things change but some things don't change. There are fantastic, hypnotic traces of the past. I love that. I love the traces.

KM

How do you feel about time? Are the past and the present all the same to you, at least in your poems?

HW

That is something else I learned from Neil: the idea of flatness that Japanese prints have. A typical line of his might be, "His jaw cuts an angle from the plantation palms." And that kind of line might also be a metaphor for time. That childhood life exists in the same plane as the adult life.

Kathryn Maris's second poetry collection is God Loves You *(Seren, 2013). Her interviews with Billy Collins and Christopher Reid appeared in* Poetry London.

Poems from *Poetry*
selected by Don Share
editor of *Poetry* and
Maurice Riordan

LOUISE GLÜCK

Aboriginal Landscape

You're stepping on your father, my mother said,
and indeed I was standing exactly in the center
of a bed of grass, mown so neatly it could have been
my father's grave, although there was no stone saying so.

You're stepping on your father, she repeated,
louder this time, which began to be strange to me,
since she was dead herself; even the doctor had admitted it.

I moved slightly to the side, to where
my father ended and my mother began.

The cemetery was silent. Wind blew through the trees;
I could hear, very faintly, sounds of weeping several rows away,
and beyond that, a dog wailing.

At length these sounds abated. It crossed my mind
I had no memory of being driven here,
to what now seemed a cemetery, though it could have been
a cemetery in my mind only; perhaps it was a park, or if not a park,
a garden or bower, perfumed, I now realized, with the scent of roses –
douceur de vivre filling the air, the sweetness of living,
as the saying goes. At some point,

it occurred to me I was alone.
Where had the others gone,
my cousins and sister, Caitlin and Abigail?

By now the light was fading. Where was the car
waiting to take us home?

I then began seeking for some alternative. I felt
an impatience growing in me, approaching, I would say, anxiety.
Finally, in the distance, I made out a small train,
stopped, it seemed, behind some foliage, the conductor
lingering against a doorframe, smoking a cigarette.

Do not forget me, I cried, running now
over many plots, many mothers and fathers –

Do not forget me, I cried, when at last I reached him.
Madam, he said, pointing to the tracks,
surely you realize this is the end, the tracks do not go further.
His words were harsh, and yet his eyes were kind;
this encouraged me to press my case harder.
But they go back, I said, and I remarked
their sturdiness, as though they had many such returns ahead of them.

You know, he said, our work is difficult: we confront
much sorrow and disappointment.
He gazed at me with increasing frankness.
I was like you once, he added, in love with turbulence.

Now I spoke as to an old friend:
What of you, I said, since he was free to leave,
have you no wish to go home,
to see the city again?

This is my home, he said.
The city – the city is where I disappear.

NATE MARSHALL

praise song

praise the Hennessy, the brown
shine, the dull burn. praise
the dare, the *take it*, the no face
you're supposed to make.
praise the house, its many rooms,
hardwood and butter leather couches;
its richness. praise the rich, their friendship.
praise the friends: the child of the well off,
the child of the well off, the child of well,
the child of welfare, the child of welfare.
praise the diversity but praise the Hennessy,
and again,   and again.   praise
the new year upon us. praise my stumble,
the shaky eye, the fluid arm, but the steady
hand. praise my hand, the burning it has.
praise the dive into the gut of a friend; the dousing
of my hand in his ribs. praise the softness of skin,
the way it always gives.

praise the pulling, the calming down.

praise the *fuck that*, the jump back into all
five of my friends fist first. praise all
five of my friends pinning me into the thick
carpet, knees in my back. praise my back,
how it hurts and raises anyway, how it flips,
how it's the best friend of my fists.
praise the swinging pool cue, how it whips
air like a disobedient child, praise the disobedient
and all the chilling   i won't do.
praise the child smile on my face, the fun
plunging a knee into a cheek of my best friend.

praise his blood, the brightness of it, a sun i bask in.
praise my blood, the nose flowing wild with effort,
the mess and taste of it, praise the swallowing,
salt and its sweetness.

praise the morning, the impossible blue,
Midwestern January above us. praise
the blues dulled in my denim by all
the brown. praise the brown shine, the dull
burn.

praise all six in my jeans, our salt
and life sitting dry on my thighs
mixing, refusing to wash away.

ANGE MLINKO

Escape Architecture

They sang Green, Green Grass of Home
sailing west from New Orleans.
They sang Ne Me Quitte Pas beneath mesquite

while digging graves in Matagorda.
Pelican soup was a vile, greasy potage.
They sang Green, Green Grass of Home

where alligator was a luxury (the meat)
down at the Turtle Bayou Turnaround.
They sang Ne Me Quitte Pas beneath mesquite.

Near the Old and Lost River they surmised
Spanish moss strains coffee pretty good.
They sang Green, Green Grass of Home.

They were whingeing Stuck in Lodi,
forty Slavonians in the Big Thicket.
They sang Ne Me Quitte Pas beneath mesquite.

They cut down the trees, they sawed the blocks,
split the blocks into billets, split the billets into boards.
They sang Green, Green Grass of Home.
They sang Ne Me Quitte Pas beneath mesquite.

·

Frederick Olmsted was right when he wrote
G.T.T. (Gone to Texas) was appended
"to every man's name who had disappeared

before the discovery of some rascality."
Brands were a language: Shanghai M, Running W.
Frederick Olmsted was right when he wrote,

or rode upright, through "a sort of Brobdingnag grass."
Bradded L, Walking R, Swinging J.
Every man's name who had disappeared

singed like needles off a cactus, whiskers off rope
(this was a practice). Rocking T, Tumbling K –
Frederick Olmsted was right when he wrote

in the alphabet we got from the Canaanites.
Oxhead A. Camel G. If it doesn't brand, it bites.
To every man's name who had disappeared,

someone added: Sent to heaven to hunt for a harp.
Or maybe it was another case of slow.
Olmsted slowed so he could write while he rode
among men whose names had disappeared.

HANNAH GAMBLE

Growing a Bear

Growing a bear – a midnight occupation,
the need for which you perhaps first realized
when you saw the wrong kind of shadow

under your chin – a convex when you expected
concave, so now it's clear
you're getting older. Your wife was in the shower

and you wanted to step inside
and soap her up like you did in college when she said

"I'll shower with you, but I'm leaving
my underwear on," and you enjoyed her
in every way you could enjoy a person with soap.

You didn't join your wife in the shower.
She's gotten funny about letting you see her
shave her legs or wash herself anywhere.

You think she read it somewhere –
that letting your husband see you pluck anything,
trim anything, apply medicine to anything,
will make him feel like he's furniture.

It's exactly on cold nights like these that the basement
is not as forbidding as it should be, despite the fact
that you have to put gloves on
in what is part of your own home.

Downstairs, a large bathtub, kept, for some reason,
after remodeling. It is there that your bear will be grown,
by you, though you have no idea how. Probably wishing

is most of it; fertilizer, chunks of raw stew meat,
handfuls of blackberries, two metal rakes, and a thick rug
make up the rest. Then water.

You get an e-mail from a friend late at night
saying he can't sleep. You write back
"I hope you feel sleepy soon" and think how childish
the word "sleepy" is. And you're a man,
older than most of the people you see on television.

You haven't even considered how your wife will feel
when you have finished growing your bear. You could
write a letter to her tonight, explaining how your life
was just so lacking in bear:

"Janet, it's nothing you've done –
clearly you have no possible way of supplying me with a bear
or any of the activities I might be able to enjoy
after acquiring the bear."

It might just be best
to keep the two worlds separate.
Janet clearly prefers things to be comfortable
and unchallenging. Janet soaps herself up. Janet puts herself
to bed, and you just happen to be next to her.

You go on your weekly bike ride with Mark and tell him
that you've been growing a bear. An eighteen-wheeler
flies by and he doesn't seem to hear you –
plus he's focused on the hill.

You think about how not all friends know
what each other sounds like when struggling and
breathing heavy. Past the age of college athletics,
most friends don't even know what each others' bodies
look like, flushed, tired, showering, cold.

MARCUS WICKER

Ode to Browsing the Web

Two spiky-haired Russian cats hit kick flips
on a vert ramp. The camera pans to another

pocket of the room where six kids rocking holey
T-shirts etch aerosol lines on warehouse walls

in words I cannot comprehend. All of this
happening in a time no older than your last

heartbeat. I've been told the internet is
an unholy place – an endless intangible

stumbling ground of false deities
dogma and loneliness, sad as a pile of shit

in a world without flies. My loneliness exists
in every afterthought. Yesterday, I watched

a neighbor braid intricate waves of cornrows
into her son's tiny head and could have lived

in her focus-wrinkled brow for a living. Today
I think I practice the religion of blinking too much.

Today, I know no neighbor's name and won't
know if I like it or not. O holy streaming screen

of counterculture punks, linger my lit mind
on landing strips – through fog, rain, hail –

without care for time or density. O world
wide web, o viral video, o god of excrement

thought. Befriend me. Be fucking infectious.
Move my eyes from one sight to the next.

C.A. CONRAD

Lonely Deep Affection

years of practice for a soft
landing in the slaughter
we looked far off to
a flag sewn into flesh
dear enemy come down the
hill I have taken a title out
of the love for you jumping
down the clear shaft of your eye
you would not know how long I
paused when writing this unless
I said so in the poem
half an hour staring
at the pencil having
written of my enemy with
love and fight to maintain
the ascension
voices from a
room no one exits
we pry genocide out
of the museum but
meant to remove
the museum
from genocide

EILEEN MYLES

Prophesy

I'm playing with the devil's cock
it's like a crayon
it's like a fat burnt crayon
I'm writing a poem with it
I'm writing that down
all that rattling heat in this room
I'm using that
I'm using that tingling rattle
that light in the middle of the room
it's my host
I've always been afraid of you
scared you're god and something else
I'm afraid when you're yellow
tawny
white it's okay. Transparent cool
you don't look like home
my belly is homeless
flopping over the waist of my jeans like an omelette
there better be something about feeling fat
what there really is is a lack of emptiness
I'm aiming for that empty feeling
going to get some of that
and then I'll be back

TOMÁS Q. MORÍN

Stanza

Because in medieval Italian it meant "room"
I tied the curtains at their elbows with
what could have been honor cords or worse
yet, a belt from the 60s, so hideous were the
tassels that were dancing a little tarantella
after I had propped the windows and the wind
had carried in the song the rubbing trees
were making, without any accompaniment,
mind you, from a tambourine, although the bells
of the occasional sleigh played that part,
while I waited for the vixen and their shameless
yelping to follow the music and the cold
and the night inside where I sat half man,
half snow, to investigate my squeaking
pencil and the flapping of the bird-white page
I couldn't seem to catch in those years when I
lugged around a frozen heart and was infatuated
with whiteness, since I had read somewhere it was
the absence of color, which could not be true
since I had once loved a pure white duck with
a white bill and feet and I had even torn its white
flesh with my teeth that were still then white,
which should have been all the proof anyone needed
to debunk our outdated theories of absence.

MICHAEL DICKMAN

Where We Live
for John Guare

I used to live
in a mother now I live
in a sunflower

Blinded by the silverware

Blinded by the refrigerator

I sit on a sidewalk
in the sunflower and its yellow
downpour

The light of the world
beads up on one perfect
green leaf

It scribbles its name on every living thing then erases it so what's
    left is more of a whisper than a mother

Here it's spring

Over and over and over again

                    •

I used to live
in a cloud now I live
in a crow

It's tiny and crippled in there but I can find my way to the bathroom
    in the dark if I need to

All the windows
in the crow are left open
and let the clouds in

Back in

They float past my bed and have nothing to say

Hello it's nice to meet you!

From a telephone pole
tongues slide out singing
welcome home

Welcome home they sing

•

I used to live
in a tree now I live
in a king

He waves his arms in front of him and endless migrations of birds
    disappear into his coat

I like to sit up inside
his crown eating sandwiches
and watching tv

Hills shake in the distance when he shuffles his feet
Floods when he snaps his fingers

I bow inside his brow and the afternoon stretches out
Orders more sandwiches

And sells the slaves

and sets the slaves free

and sells the slaves

PATRICIA LOCKWOOD

The Hypno-Domme Speaks, and Speaks and Speaks

I was born as a woman, I talk you to death,
      or else your ear off,
or else you to sleep. What do I have, all the time
in the world, and a voice that swings brass back
and forth, you can hear it, and a focal point where
my face should be. What do I have, I have absolute
power, and what I want is your money, your drool,
and your mind, and the sense of myself as a snake,
and a garter in the grass. Every bone in the snake
is the hipbone, every part of the snake is the hips.
The first sound I make is silence, then sssssshhh,
  the first word I say is listen. Sheep shearers
   and accountants hypnotize the hardest,
and lookout sailors who watch the sea, and the boys
who cut and cut and cut and cut and cut the grass.
The writers who write page-turners, and the writers
who repeat themselves. The diamond-cutter kneels
down before me and asks me to hypnotize him, and
I glisten at him and glisten hard, and listen to me and
listen, I tell him. Count your age backward, I tell him.
Become aware of your breathing, and aware of mine
   which will go on longer. Believe you
  are a baby till I tell you otherwise, then believe
you're a man till I tell you you're dirt. When a gunshot
rings out you'll lie down like you're dead. When you
  hear, "He is breathing," you'll stand up again.
The best dog of the language is Yes and protects you.
The best black-and-white dog of the language is Yes
and goes wherever you go, and you go where I say,
you go anywhere. Why do I do it is easy, I am working
my way through school. Give me the money
   for Modernism, and give me the money

for what comes next. When you wake to the fact that you
have a body, you will wake to the fact that not for long.
When you wake you will come when you read the word
hard, or hard to understand me, or impenetrable poetry.
When you put down the book you will come when you
hear the words put down the book,

                  you will come when you hear.

LEAH UMANSKY

Khaleesi Says
Game of Thrones

In this story, she is fire-born:
knee-deep in the shuddering world.

In this story, she knows no fear,
for what is fractured is a near-bitten star,
a false-bearing tree,
or a dishonest wind.

In this story, fear is a house gone dry.
Fear is *not* being a woman.

I'm no ordinary woman, she says.
My dreams come true.

And she says and she is
and I say, *yes, give me that.*

ADAM FITZGERALD

Time After Time
after Cyndi Lauper

I'm in the barricade hearing the clock thickening you.
    Autumn encircles a confusion that's nothing new.
Flash back to warring eyes almost letting me drown.

Out of which, a picture of me walking in a foreign head.
    I can't hear what you said. Then you say: Cold room,
the second that life unwinds. A tinctured vase returns

to grass. Secrets doled out deep inside a drum beat out
    of time. Whatever you said was ghostly slow like
a second hand unwinding by match light. Lying back

to the wheel, I shirked confusion. You already knew.
    Suitcases surround me. You picture me too far ahead.
Yet I can't hear what you've said. You say: Doldrums,

some secondhand wine. Love, you knew my precincts.
    The stone house turned out black, the scenic tunics
were deep inside. Who said home? Oh, I fall behind.

That very secret height blinds. Lying like a diamond,
    the cock-thickening of you: hunchbacked arms, eyes
left behind. You'll picture me walking far, far ahead.

I hear what you've done. You said: Go slow. I feebly
    bleed out. Matthew's sermon turned out to be glass.
I wander in windows soft as Sour Patch. No rewind.

But something is out of touch and you, you're Sinbad.
    That second date totally mine. Lying in a vacuum,
the thickening plot thinks of you. The future's not new.

TOUCHDOWN. Lights. All those celebrity behinds.
    A suitcase full of weeds. You picture me coming to.
You: too close to me to hear what you've already said.

Then you say: The second wind unwinds. Doves whistle,
    halving their dovely backs, watching out windows to see
if I'm okay. See it, the dulcet moment? I'm like thicket

tinkering for you. Fusion nothing you knew. Flash back
    to seagull-beguiled eyes. Sometimes talking to a barren
lad. Such music so unbearably droll. The hand is mine.

Random picture frames off the darkness. A Turing machine?
    Scotch-taping through windows, stolen from deep inside
rum-beaded thyme. You say also: Behind sequins & hinds...

And I'm in the barricade hearing the clock thickening you.
    Clematis enclosures, walking with news, pollinated by a
secondary grief, while something reminds you of our love.

MICHAEL ROBBINS

Not Fade Away

Half of the Beatles have fallen
and half are yet to fall.
Keith Moon has set. Hank Williams
hasn't answered yet.

Children sing for Alex Chilton.
Whitney Houston's left the Hilton.
Hendrix, Guru, Bonham, Janis.
They have a tendency to vanish.

Bolan, Bell, and Boon by car.
How I wonder where they are.
Hell is now Jeff Hanneman's.
Adam Yauch and three Ramones.

[This space held in reserve
for Zimmerman and Osterberg,
for Bruce and Neil and Keith,
that sere and yellow leaf.]

Johnny Cash and Waylon Jennings,
Stinson, Sterling, Otis Redding.
Johnny Thunders and Joe Strummer,
Ronnie Dio, Donna Summer.

Randy Rhoads and Kurt Cobain,
Patsy Cline and Ronnie Lane.
Poly Styrene, Teena Marie.
Timor mortis conturbat me.

OCEAN VUONG

Aubade with Burning City

South Vietnam, April 29, 1975: Armed Forces Radio played Irving Berlin's 'White Christmas' as a code to begin Operation Frequent Wind, the ultimate evacuation of American civilians and Vietnamese refugees by helicopter during the fall of Saigon.

> Milkflower petals on the street
> > like pieces of a girl's dress.

May your days be merry and bright...

He fills a teacup with champagne, brings it to her lips.
> *Open*, he says.
> > She opens.
> > > Outside, a soldier spits out
> his cigarette as footsteps
> > fill the square like stones fallen from the sky. *May all*
> > > *your Christmases be white* as the traffic guard
> unstraps his holster.

> > His hand running the hem
of her white dress.
> > His black eyes.
> Her black hair.
> > A single candle.
> > Their shadows: two wicks.

A military truck speeds through the intersection, the sound of children
> > shrieking inside. A bicycle hurled
> through a store window. When the dust rises, a black dog
> > lies in the road, panting. Its hind legs
> > > crushed into the shine
> > *of a white Christmas.*

On the nightstand, a sprig of magnolia expands like a secret heard
for the first time.

The treetops glisten and children listen, the chief of police
facedown in a pool of Coca-Cola.
A palm-sized photo of his father soaking
beside his left ear.

The song moving through the city like a widow.
A white... A white... I'm dreaming of a curtain of snow

falling from her shoulders.

Snow crackling against the window. Snow shredded

with gunfire. Red sky.
Snow on the tanks rolling over the city walls.
A helicopter lifting the living just out of reach.

The city so white it is ready for ink.

The radio saying run run run.
Milkflower petals on a black dog
like pieces of a girl's dress.

May your days be merry and bright. She is saying
something neither of them can hear. The hotel rocks
beneath them. The bed a field of ice
cracking.

Don't worry, he says, as the first bomb brightens
their faces, *my brothers have won the war
and tomorrow...*
The lights go out.

I'm dreaming. I'm dreaming...
              to hear sleigh bells in the snow ...

In the square below: a nun, on fire,
              runs silently toward her god –

        Open, he says.
                She opens.

Essay

THE LEGACY OF GOTTFRIED BENN
Eva Bourke

In his only television interview, on the occasion of his seventieth birthday in 1956 and shortly before his death, Dr Gottfried Benn, dermatologist, specialist for venereal diseases and famous German poet, emphasised how much Berlin meant to him: "Berlin is the city that formed me," he said. "This is where I studied and became someone. I experienced Berlin in its heyday up to 1933 when it was on the verge of taking its place alongside Paris as a centre of the intellect and arts in Europe, wonderful years, a wealth of talent in theatre, music, literature that was unique. People streamed from all over the world to the city." Benn failed to mention, however, that by 1933 he had already compromised himself by his ill-fated involvement with the Nazis, the very people who later set about the destruction of his beloved Berlin. In 1932 he had been elected to the literature section of the Prussian Academy of the Arts, an honour he shared with literary greats such as Thomas and Heinrich Mann, Ricarda Huch, Alfred Döblin. In a manoeuvre to silence potential critics among the literati, the Nazis put pressure on the academy to abolish its democratic statutes. Benn belonged to the wing of nationalist-conservative members – he never bothered to conceal his contempt for democracy, civilization and humanist ideals, and in April 1933 publicly dismissed "the old liberal values and persons" in a blatantly pro-Nazi radio talk on 'The New State and the Intellectuals' – drafted a letter to Goebbels assuring the new powers of the academy's loyalty. Possibly this was a ruse in order to preserve some of the academy's autonomy but it back-fired. When he demanded that all put their names to this letter many of the luminaries resigned from the academy on the spot and several went into exile.

Thomas Mann's son, Klaus, an ardent admirer of Benn, wrote an impassioned letter asking him why he hadn't also left the academy but instead had sided with people whose "moral depravity was abhorrent to the rest of the world". He pointed out to Benn that his radicalism of language would antagonise the Nazis, adding "if I am not a bad prophet you will reap no more than thanklessness and scorn". Benn's disgraceful reply not only to Mann but also to other criticism voiced against him by exiles appeared in the form of a public address in a newspaper. Perhaps this was pre-emptive, a stubborn refusal to recant, perhaps he was jealous of the exiles sitting pretty on "sunny French beaches". But of course Mann was right; Benn's specific mixture of drastic description and expressionism was anathema to the Nazis. It wasn't long before he was attacked, branded as *entartet* (degenerate), and finally banned from writing or publishing in 1938. Benn withdrew from actual personal danger into the army, "the aristocratic form of exile", as he put it. As a military doctor he could re-enlist any time, and ironically he managed to spend peaceful and productive years stationed in the quiet city of Hanover. Much later, in 1950, he admitted that Klaus Mann, "this 27-year-old", had been more clear-sighted about the situation than he had been.

The Benn reception in Germany has had to wrestle with this legacy. Benn didn't hold back with his anti-democratic views but blithely put sign-posts all over his writings; his essay 'Eugenics' for instance – the German *Züchtung* means breeding in the biological sense and has an unsettlingly close etymological relationship with *Züchtigung*, i.e. punishment – extols a Nietzschean ideal, the birth of New Man, a mystical, quasi-religious renewal of the 'Volk', what his biographer Fritz J. Raddatz describes as Benn's anti-humanist hymn of elitism, intoxication and eugenics. He was no misled or seduced intellectual, he never retracted his views but stuck with them till the end. They reflected the pessimistic mood prevailing among intellectuals in Europe after the First World War, of imminent doom, the collapse of civilizations and the necessity of a rebirth under the aegis of a racial or aristocratic elite – and in this he was close in spirit to other reactionary poets, such as Yeats, Eliot and Pound. He placed art as a form of aesthetic ersatz religion above everything – it was demonic and mysterious, transcendental, and superseded moral values, social concerns, commerce and politics. He had, however, been mistaken in his belief that the new rulers would embrace this religion. They hated his expressionist poetry, the *Morgue* poems, literary equivalents of the bitingly satirical canvases of Otto Dix or George Grosz. Moreover, in one significant way Benn differed from the Nazis – he was never an anti-Semite, which prompted Raddatz to call him a Fascist rather than a Nazi.

Benn continues to evoke ambivalent feelings. In my old 'rororo' monograph there are black-and-white photographs of the military doctor in his lab coat or of a stocky man with deep-set melancholy eyes in the company of a beautiful woman. I recall, from reading Benn as a teenager, the smell of the cheap Limes 1968 edition in eight volumes, bound in dusty-blue linen. I understood little but fell under the spell of the unmistakable 'Benn sound': the swinging jazzy rhythms, the abrupt harshness versus the lush exotic landscapes, the seductive melancholy, world-weariness, the flippancy and pure *chuzpe* of his style, the wild mix of shreds of talk, news, medical facts:

> O blond! O summer of that nape. O
> Jessamine-drenched pulse-points.
> I am fond of you. I stroke
> Your shoulder. Let's go:
>
> Tyrrhenian Sea. A conspirative blue.
> Doric temples. The plains
> Pregnant with roses. Fields
> Die asphodel deaths.
>
> ('Englisches Café', trans. Michael Hofmann)

But I also felt overwhelmed by the hectoring arrogance, language burdened with travel brochure kitsch ("a white pearl rolls back to sea") and stanzas stuffed with bric-a-brac pilfered from Greek history, myth and art, fragments of erudition, neologisms, Graecisms (*katadyomenal*). His insistence on the "absolute poem, the poem without belief, the poem without hope, the poem addressed to no-one", seemed dated, nineteenth century to me, and I found his pronounced contempt for his fellow humans, his self-pity and frequent sentimentality off-putting:

> Eternally endless processions
> before the sinking eye,
> distant waves, evanescence –
> where do they lead us? – why,
> back to the cries' decrescendo,
> to the hemlock, the end of light,
> but a step lamentando
> to the urn of the night.
>
> ('Banana', trans. David Paisey)

Alfred Döblin, author of *Berlin Alexanderplatz* and academy ex-colleague, said that Benn's poetry was "urological, cosmic, prehistoric, erudite and largely incomprehensible". He could have added anti-rational, nihilist, esoteric, cynical. And yet with equal justification one could draw up another list of adjectives: casual, musical, seductive, humorous, sensual, earthy, primal, laconic and, especially in his later work, even compassionate and humane. The tug and pull of Benn's poetry in opposite directions has a physical effect on the reader unlike any other. It is more of an assault on the body, the senses, oscillating between extremes of hot and cold, harsh and soft, soporific and electrifying, and it should come with a health warning.

In the 70s at Munich University I attended a graduate seminar on Benn. Much of the seminar was taken up with lengthy discussions on methodological approaches. My work group decided on the purely linguistic structuralist method. I have forgotten if we got anywhere with it but the fact that it was empirical, non-speculative and focused on aspects of language must have had to do with this choice – it let us off the hook, we didn't have to confront the meaning and the ideological undercurrent of the poems or the poet's compromised past. As a result I found myself skipping through the work counting and classifying flowers. I discovered he didn't exactly look at plants – they were just part of the lyrical furniture, mood signifiers. During this agitated, politicised decade after Brecht had replaced Benn as *poeta primus inter pares,* or as someone put it, after the Janus head of German poetry had turned around again, his influence waned; nevertheless he continued to hang in there. Marcel Reich-Ranitzky remarked a few years ago, when asked if there was a Benn renaissance happening in Germany around the 2006 anniversaries of his birth and death, there was no need for a renaissance because Benn had never gone away. In 1999 the influential poetry journal *DAS GEDICHT* (the poem) had drawn up a list of the ten most illustrious poets of the century in Germany and, surprisingly, Benn was voted number one by the jury, followed by Celan, Brecht, Rilke, Trakl, Bachmann; Hans Magnus Enzensberger, who himself didn't much like Benn, calling his poetry "jagged and rusty", his prose "woolly and muddily phrased", only finished tenth. Whatever you may think of such literary *Top of the Pops*, it proves that readers increasingly distinguish between the often ill-judged politics of the poet and the poetry.

In the *Encyclopedia of Literary Translations into English* (2000), Ian Hilton writes that Benn still needed to be introduced to English language readers. I suspect that Benn's political reputation got in the way in Britain and that, in Hilton's words, Benn's short-lived yet markedly sympathetic identification with Nazism had "duly heaped embarrassment and opprobrium upon his head". There had been one major selection of his writings, *Primal Vision*, edited by E.B. Ashton in 1958, and little else since. *Primal Vision* featured 32 poems in English, translated by, among others, Michael Hamburger and Christopher Middleton, and the rest were excerpts from the prose writings. It was a pioneering venture – even if the translations were "cumbrous, starchy and muted" according to Michael Hofmann. The book, however, generally fell by the wayside or was dismissed. Some English poets like John Heath-Stubbs decided that "all this thing about 'Artistik' was out of date".

The two recent publications of Benn's work in English, *Impromptus*, translated by Michael Hofmann[1] and *Selected Poems and Prose*, translated by David Paisey,[2] constitute a complete reversal of fortunes for the Benn reception. Anyone with serious interest in Benn will be delighted, and should read both books in order to get a more comprehensive idea of him and the almost unsurmountable obstacles any translator of his work faces. The Paisey and Hofmann selections complement each other as if this had been pre-arranged: they show two quite different sides of the poet. In his lucid introduction to *Impromptus*, Hofmann explains his choices, for

1. Gottfried Benn, Impromptus: Selected Poems, *edited and translated by Michael Hofmann (Faber, 2014).*

2. Gottfried Benn, Selected Poems and Prose, *edited and translated by David Paisey (Carcanet, 2013).*

example why he opted mostly for the free verse poems. They are mainly taken from the early expressionist *Morgue* poems, from those written after 1947 and from the posthumous poems with a noticeable gap in the middle. The years from 1922 to 1936 are represented by only four poems, and from 1937 to 1947 by seven. Hofmann doesn't dismiss the poems of the middle period – "there are ferocious energies at work within them," he says – but "they were too difficult and idiosyncratic for me to carry them into English in any important way. I preferred to go, more or less straight, from the shocking early to the weary late: to those beerily misanthropic and magically beautiful mutterings of Benn's last two decades. [...] They come with their own silence and space."

By coincidence many of the "beautiful, bizarre and barely translatable" (Hofmann) poems of the middle years can be found in the Paisey collection. Paisey had begun his life-long involvement with Benn as a young man when he wrote an MA thesis on the poet. He visited him in Berlin in 1955 and recalls that Benn was very kind to a painfully inexperienced student. Paisey bravely meets the challenge of those intractable poems, trying to stick to the metric and rhyming structures throughout, an almost impossible task. He concedes that his "efforts may be futile, but I think, there may be some merit in trying to convey something of the quality of a great poet to Anglophone readers who cannot read him in the original". He has been largely successful in this, although some of the solutions are awkward or hard to follow – why for instance translate the beautifully musical *Meere – Leere*, as *pampas – blankness*? It is clumsy as a rhyme, of a different register and *blankness* is not even vaguely equivalent to the notion of an existential void or of vast empty spaces conjured up by *Leere*. There are other such examples. However, the pros outweigh such quibbles. Paisey's book is a valuable and comprehensive guided tour through the poems' intricate labyrinth of references, darknesses and flashes of brilliance, and it comes with the German originals.

Benn, as the kind of idiosyncratic poet he was, naturally invited imitators and parodists – another form of translation. Recently I came across a poem entitled 'dr. bierfahrer' (dr. drayman) parodying 'Little Aster' from Benn's first collection *Morgue* (1912):

A drowned drayman was hoisted on to the slab.
Someone had jammed a lavender aster
between his teeth.

As I made the incision up from the chest
with the long blade
under the skin
to cut out tongue and palate,
I must have nudged it because it slipped
into the brain lying adjacent.
I packed it into the thorax
with the excelsior
when he was sewn up.
Drink your fill in your vase!
Rest easy,
little aster!

('Little Aster', trans. Hofmann)

The parody quoted below wittily illustrates the dilemma facing Benn readers in Germany. According to the commentary by Ulrich Bergmann, he had found it handwritten on a piece of paper stuck between the pages of the 1960 Limes edition which he just purchased in the pedestrian zone of Bad Godesberg: *under the dissecting table / he had hoisted / the much-cited body onto / we found him / instead of a heart / a whopping aster / beat in his breast / his skull was packed / with masses / of sterile excelsior / and between his teeth / someone had stuck / a lavender swastika / it wasn't a pretty sight!*

In his work as well as in life Benn could appear aloof, an outsider and observer, on occasion even distant and cold. But there is another aspect to his personality that emerges from many of the later poems in *Impromptus*. They display the grudging humanity, capable of humour and compassion, and the tenderness of an aging loner who has been through a lot and is no longer sure what it all meant. "Two world wars, two marriages, two bereavements, careers in the military and medicine, and forty years of writing have gone into their making" (Hofmann). Some late poems spell out in simple clear diction his astonishment at the discovery that other people are human, too, something that is naturally obvious to most:

I have often asked myself and never found an answer
whence kindness and gentleness come,
I don't know it to this day, and now must go myself.

('People Met', trans. Hofmann)

Hofmann, himself a brilliant English poet of German descent and an experienced, skilful translator of German language poetry and prose, is in an excellent position to bring English-language readers closer to Benn or vice versa. He has achieved the near-impossible with these translations – there's not a whiff of 'translatorese', they read like English originals, playful, supple, stylish, the lines sparkling with wit. Hofmann is such a virtuoso he almost goes overboard from sheer exuberance, yet the overall impression is one of perfect control and forcefulness. Benn couldn't be better served than by someone who can rhyme pundits with *pour le mérite*. And in the lovely poem 'Asters', Hofmann gives the lyrical moment enough breathing space with just a touch of slant rhyme or assonance here and there, rather than forcing the musical lines into a strict rhyme scheme:

Asters – sweltering days
Old adjuration / curse,
The gods hold the balance
For an uncertain hour.

Once more the golden flocks
Of heaven, the light, the trim –
What is the ancient process
Hatching under its dying wings?

Once more the yearned-for,
The intoxication, the rose of you,
Summer leaned in the doorway
Watching the swallows.

One more presentiment
Where certainty is not hard to come by:
Wing tips brush the face of the waters,
Swallows sip speed and night.

Eva Bourke was born in Germany and lives in Ireland. Her most recent collection is Piano *(Dedalus, 2011).*

JOHN HARTLEY WILLIAMS

The Swimming Pool at Tönning

Behind the dam across the Eider river
the estuary is three miles wide. A great
construction bars the flood of North Sea tides
that batter at its iron gates. Upstream,
seals slump on sandbanks, sheep graze meadows
lusher than the saturated sky; Arctic Tern
bring fish catch to their young. Continue
on the dike path by the river till
the single spire of Tönning hoves in view.
You can take a mudbath here, wade
into the rich absorbing wallow, feel
your feet glide in, the brilliant slough
accept you. For those whose temperament
abjures a slosh, a swimming pool invites.
Salty water, blue and filtered, awaits
your jump. Got your spa card?
Taxes paid? Dive in. Get wet. Enjoy.

You're not the only swimmer. Observe
that white-haired man of eighty swim two lengths
then stop to trade an insult and a joke
with the lady who is lifeguard and cashier
and server at the café counter where
the choice is several sorts of ice
or a plastic beaker full of acid coffee.
Fourteen and chubby, half-submerged,
two girls practise kissing mouth to mouth.
A gang of boys is laughing, though at what
it's hard to say. From the highest diving board
more lads hurl themselves into the water;
as one goes down another takes a run
and follows, missing him by inches.

The lifeguard screeches from her windowed cubicle
but boys like jumping, girls like
kissing; the sun dictates from zenith.

On a bench three ladies sit and sip
their blood-undoing brew, and talk, and talk.
There's more to talk about in Tönning
than you might think. A man in jeans
and T-shirt, his brown arms dense with wiry hair,
the tip of a baroque tattoo just visible
between his shirt hem and bravado belt,
stops to add a little to what's said and
everyone is laughing. There's a lot to laugh at
here in Tönning. Conspiracies
unravel while you plough your furrow
back and forth; your head bobs up with
every stroke in time to catch what follows.
Good thing you thought to bring your goggles,
somewhat smeary, true, but through them
you see faces changing with the voltage of surprise
to hear the school director and a pupil have eloped.

You've nearly done your twenty lengths.
You like this town. You like its photogenic mayor,
his squint-eyed deputy who's clearly hatching plots,
the business plans of lawyer Hollergreve.
You admire the bearded benefactor's bust –
the man who built the pool in 1927
and founded Tönning Swimming Club and built
the fine hotel. The posters in the lobby for
the long departed circus and the pastor's fund
to cure the spire's kink engage your revery.

You feel a kinship with the passion of the skinny youth
who dreams of leaving Tönning and doesn't realise
the girl beside him has got plans for him
and all of this beside a river full of mud,
incomparable, shiny, slicky, health-bestowing mud,
that curves into a distance live with gulls,
three miles wide across, gleaming under heaven.

Benders

Knees are the only friends you have.
When you lie down, tired on a bed,
they crouch quietly, like faithful knights at a distance.
Move, and they're ready to go with you.

Knees are what keep you
well out in front, their skin breaking into scars
across the pebbly roundedness
of bone, like surf on shingle.

Should a new aesthetic sweep the nation,
oblivious to fashion, they'll keep going.
Deaf, they cannot hear the 'View Halloo!'
Blind, they cannot see the crimson faces in pursuit.

Cornered, your knees will drop you in a culvert,
while you engage the enemy
by showing trapped civility.
Whatever you do, don't bark.

Ahead, you glimpse the sweet scamper
of vanishing truth. She disappears with a flash of tail
into the corn. The hounds give vent to their belling cry.
This is the moment you crank your humble benders

and surprise them all, in sprinting pursuit of she who,
ruse, feint and double-back though she may be,
now has your knees to reckon with, that straight ahead crookedness
they do so well, recovering, dodging and veering on,

as they race you over the fields of your health
while you strive to grasp your destination.
Ignore those brutes, the vodka-puffed cheeks behind you.
Wherever your knees propel you,

it isn't logic that drives them. And they won't rest
till you stand before the fair embodiment
of the reason for your swiftness. Seeing as
you're so much ahead of the pack – how can you fail?

KATRINA NAOMI

Elemental

I shouldn't have lied when you asked about the mud.
Had I told you I press a cleat from the boots of the men
who walk up from the village, you might have found this odd.
While they sleep, I bend each sole until a wedge of packed earth
falls onto my palm. Something from the outside, coming in.

Had you pulled the curtain, you'd have seen a jar
of my Nan's hair, woollen in its whiteness.
I used to free the wisps from the comb's tines with forefinger
and thumb; poke out with a pin the dark of the gunk and grease.
Had you asked, you might have found this strange.

And had you moved the jar, looked, further back,
you'd have seen a tin of glass and small, sharp stones
gouged from the tyres of my Dad's Austin Traveller.
Like an occupation, just something I did, sat on the kerb,
cradling rubber; my very first touch of a screwdriver.

You can shake the tin, it's all there. I'm more selective,
now, in my choice of chevrons, zig-zags and tubes of soil.
I don't clean their boots, that would admit a form of love,
but lay each treasure in a Perspex dish, something elemental,
and you might say, bordering on the forensic.

SIMON RICHEY

A History of the Tongue

It lay idle on the beds of their mouths,
or came to life along a length of bone,
or on another's body;

and in time folded itself into a runnel
for a sound to pass through,
again and again;

and then fluttered for the sheer pleasure of it
in the wind of their breathing,
words rising from them like birds.

One

In this primitive, magical state... everything participated in everything else.
   – Erich Neumann, The Origins and History of Consciousness

There were no words then
to make one thing
into two. The trees
were still embedded

in the sky, and the rivers
and the river banks
and the birds that gathered there
ran into one another.

A whole people
would cry out as one,
or feel aggrieved as one,
and laughter could fill a wood.

MARTHA KAPOS

The Magnetic Field

Aloof and entire on the pillow
your white-washed face lifted up
almost too high to reach

and all the cardinal points of your body
laid out on this bed we didn't make
became a silent spectacle

arranged on a bare mahogany table
at the back of a long hushed room at school
to teach us magnetism.

Pigeons tapping their heads in the yard
stems of grass, the small sunlit gravel
beyond the half-opened shutters

were stopped in the furious
speed of their lives until
statements of fact as slight

as the sound of cutlery on plates
heard from a distant window
were folded in around your hands

until tall blocks of cloud
edged forward to form an audience
until faint trails of skywriting

gathered in swathes and drew
the entire minor contents of Massachusetts
into a circumference

its patterned slopes and valleys
its airy streets
a paper napkin floating in a puddle

all stood arranged in a series
of fine concentric circles to petal
and fan from your head and feet.

Homecoming
i.m. S.V.

While we stood and raised our glasses
you stepped out of your clothes.
Your face slid from our thoughts as headfirst
you bowed and went deep
into the warm pond where the water

moves inevitably under its lid
still as a box and there you are
the same length as the water
whiskered and white rolling onto your back
a sleepy dogfish basking along the bottom

where it's dark in the spacious mud
eyeing up the distant
undersides of algae and transparent green lily pads
the numerous flies pulling in tightly together
humming a low riff over the water

while Burl Ives comes in with
Jimmy crack corn and I don't care
under the hot clouds and long blue days of summer
when Florida was like no place on earth.

VICKI FEAVER

Pugilist

Uncle who was killed in the War;
whose boxing gloves, stitched
from padded orange leather,
were stored in the cupboard
above my bed; who haunted

our house, making my father
feel guilty for not fighting
and dying and stopping
my mother and grandmother
from ever being happy.

On Remembrance Day,
when they sat behind green
velvet curtains, watching
a tiny black-and-white telly
and weeping as poppy wreaths

were laid on the cenotaph,
I sneaked out of the lounge
to dance on the lawn, paper poppy
pinned in my hair, leaping
and twirling in wet grass.

That night, Uncle Jack
appeared in my dream –
jigging from foot to foot,
throwing punches at me
with bunched orange fists.

I woke with a nosebleed:
a flow of scarlet drops
soaking my pillow and sheets
and an old towel and half-
filling the blue kitchen bowl.

Prayer at Seventy

God of thresholds, guide
of souls between worlds,
have mercy on me

who when I asked you
if I could pass my last years
with less anxiety

changed me into a tiny spider
launching into the unknown
on a thread of gossamer

and when I begged you
to let me be a bigger
fiercer creature

into a polar bear
leaping between
melting ice flows.

MARTHA SPRACKLAND

Visit

In an early memory the woman who is my namesake
comes to visit from New Zealand. It was during those years
I was forever taking my clothes off – at the shops, school,
the houses of other people – and when she arrived
into the garden I was in the knuckled plum tree, naked
and monkeyish, knocking the green plums to the ground.
If there were words, I have forgotten them.
Probably she said Well hello in that way people have
of talking to children, but I do remember how she stood
beneath the overladen branches with my mother, both
young and a little awkward together after all this time,
both shading their eyes with a hand and looking up
interestedly, as if having glimpsed in that blue sky
an uncommon bird passing overhead, or a cloud
shaped almost exactly like something familiar.

MEIRION JORDAN

A Mercy

Iesu, trugarha wrthyf
      – last words of Richard Gwyn, Catholic martyr, 1584

In death they spilled out like a truant's take
from those schoolmaster's pockets: Peter's keys
notched from some hard keeping; a sky of crows,
their black wings drubbing his heart awake –

though stubborn now it seemed it would not break
for all the hangman's knocking; then the sixpence
he'd once pledged the state in deference
to his several crimes. Which little joke

next to his last words sticks in the throat,
that he called for mercy as his guts were drawn
who laughing once had goosed some prissy vicar

hectoring him from the court-cum-pulpit's height.
For whose sake at last God sought to drown
death with his testament. *Iesu, trugarha.*

The ordinary state of things

for George Szirtes

In a bar
where rain pours down the walls,
the ceiling daubed
with cubist ravings of a suicide,

its one window
looking out
on a courtyard where great-aunts,
some of them six feet tall,

go to light cheap Russian cigarettes
and sit giving death the evil eye,
or Napoleon,
or whatever pipsqueak is passing,

the record player knows only
Gloomy Sunday,
and the music strikes up
with angles stranger than the door-jambs

as though a jazz band
trapped in the caved cellar
by a Soviet bomb
had forgotten to ask for their rider

or a Roma
dressed in an ancient morning-suit
was pulling the strings from his fiddle
as it neighs in disappointment –

and listening to this
in another century
on a phonograph
carved in the shape of an owl

bequeathed by a long-forgotten
Transylvanian grandmother
is the man who takes off his jacket
slowly

pours out the tea
and welcomes his guests
protesting that this, too,
is the ordinary state of things.

AMALI RODRIGO

Kama Sutra

Think of the weaver bent over the loom
in a posture of appeasement, though it is not.
He hears the beyond in him, an older voice.

Without pause or trembling, his winged
hands thread the briefer weft of cerise,
silver, through warp taut on its frame.

Though he does not pause, think of the rain
he doesn't miss, pounding on the roof,
branches of the jacaranda scratching

the windowpane like a cat impatient
to be let in. Think how they learn
to wait, as all things must,

while the foliage thickens, until a hare
finds itself startled by a star or the deer
occasionally leaping. In a quiet opening,

a hunt is taking shape. Though he doesn't
know where each turning may lead,
he adds lilies, a monkey like a go-between

among the Banyan's sky-roots, a peacock
unhooking its nerve. Think how he breathes
into them, into each knot reworked,

each new loop that shows a little more
of itself; and this archer, he sends
into the world to become an arrow.

When all the birds fly up at once
in the tapestry's very centre,
think of the barely disturbed tree.

Good Luck Goldfish

To generate the most luck, use nine fish:
eight red or golden and one black

Where there is water there is a memory
of a river, of a chalice, of a thirst
unslaked. Here, among amulets
and totems, inside a display case, the Koi
run frantic in their small silver cell
as if the force of desire could recover
the river, red flecking water, water turning
to wine. How shall I drink such blunt ardour,

such clockwork blessing. A vagrant gene
turned gold. And yet the source is present
too, a barely visible gravity we keep
arriving at, wanting happiness, exacting
its due. Finding how every paradise is walled,
we make our own way home, hearing a river near.

Meditation on Cherry Blossoms

When the first buds open in Okinawa
it is not a joy exactly.
Snow has not stopped for days.

When it does I listen
each night to the blossom forecast
and only think of snow falling.

·

On the day they told us of a change in Kumamoto
I saw how I had changed between the beginning
and the end of the sentence.

·

There are days you want to know the truth so badly
you'll trade anything for it.

When they announce the blossoming in Kyoto
I want to take it all back.

·

A bridge between one shore and the other,
the river forever trying to escape it.

This is how longings arrive; tiny buds
of resolutions that will not survive.

·

Down by the river the trees are raucous
in bloom, the wet road beneath marching
steadily towards the house.

·

Blossoms always return to the same tree.
In my dream I return to the same house
yet that road is unrecognisable.

.

Knowing true North, how lightly they travel
right through us to Nagoya.

Blindly we lie down and offer
our bones to the spaces we are made of.

.

When they began to bud in Aomori at the ocean's brink
I understood how desire has enormous scales,
is like fish leaping in our bodies.

When they began to bud in Aomori
they were also waiting to ignite in Hokkaido,
Okinawa, Aomori and for a moment

I believed I was here; I was real.

.

When they began to bud in Aomori I understood
what I am to you is a mirror
that says you are beautiful.

.

When the first blossoms appear in Hokkaido
it is like something breaking far away.

STEVE ELY

Deir ez-Zor

All the world is sleeping – hush!

Four rivers of Eden;
Hiddekel, Pison, Gihon, Euphrates.
Adamu's garden, a woman picking fruit
in the cool of evening,
unfathomed darkness of stars.

Four rivers of Al Jazirah;
Colap, Kharbur, Al Furat, Nahr Dijla.
Ashurbanipal's garden, orchard and well,
maiden awaiting her lover's sweet song.
Did he arrive? Shrikes are hunting
through the olive groves, spearing
nightingales on branches.

Jahannam's four rivers;
salt-tears, urine, diarrhoea, blood.
Zeki Bay's garden of knives.
Women cooking grass. Children
licking moisture from stones.

Work

Cutting in the cane fields
or hacking back scrub,
it was something we were used to:
after all, we were farmers.

We'd gather every morning
before setting out,
then cutting all day
in the jungle and marshes.

We'd come back exhausted,
well worthy of beer
and brochettes. Our wives
turned their backs in bed.

In those days was beef
and ribsteak in plenty.
We bore the knives ourselves:
slaughtering, jointing.

We feasted like the elegant kings
to whom were given
such bloody instructions
they jumped to the life to come.

Interhamwe

Please allow me to introduce myself,
I'm a man of wealth and taste.

The werewolf seems more were than wolf.
He's a nice guy, plausible. He's a giver.
He gives us permission. He's a liberator.
He frees us from guilt. He knows we're all sinners.
He forgives us, and we know it's alright
to forgive ourselves. He touches our hearts,
and we're called forth to testify, holding hands
with our glassy-eyed sisters and brothers.
You're never alone. You're one with those
who work together, a *team*. Were and wolf:
twin creatures of the pack.
                   St. Brice's Day,
Oxenford. Infesting the streets like cockles
among the corn, we took scythes to the plague
of Danish tares. The King decreed it; his people
made it happen.
               Clifford's Tower, with clubs
and staves. The Jews killed Christ, were rich
and stand-offish. Our reward was release and carnival.
It doesn't feel wrong when everyone's doing it.
          At St. Martin's Vintry, a Kentish ploughman
suggested the shibboleth. Jack Straw brought the axes.
The English insisted on English bread and cheese.
'*Case en brode*' was the best the Flemings could do.
They lost their heads. Wheat and chaff, sheep and goats,
us and them. Team-building via pogrom.
          But teams get results: hit sales targets,
build bridges from cardboard and paper clips;
go out on the piss and wreck the Jade Palace.

Fifteen yeomen in ripped St. George
bellowing the National Anthem. Brings a tear
to your eye. Makes you want to tear heads off.

My work here is done.

Fasayil

Yes, I remember Fasayil
the dirt-track's hanging gate
a shanty of tents and mud-brick shacks
annexed to the Jewish State.

Melon fields of blinding light
and sentried ranks of palms,
Tomer's barbed-wire cash-crops,
Fasayil's destitute farms.

The drudgery of those melon fields
was relieved by the company
of my smiling Bedouin workmates
exiled and refugee.

Yet I refused an invitation
to dine with them in their homes,
not because the Arabs will eat your heart
and make bread with your bones,

but because a Brooklyn accent
said this is the West Bank guys
and those that eat with Arabs
are terrorists and spies.

Shabbat shalom on Tomer
grilled steaks and Maccabi beer
'Dance Rock' and the Kids from Fame,
Sharon and Shamir.

Yes, I remember Fasayil
where I learned good men are meek,
and collude with power against the poor,
the dispossessed and weak.

THE YAWP OF ORALITY

Daljit Nagra, Ramayana: A Retelling, *Faber, £18.99*
ISBN 9780571294879

reviewed by Aingeal Clare

. . .

Which art form has the best modern epics, poetry or the novel? Monty Python staged a philosophers' football match between the Germans and the Greeks, and any genre grudge match between the two forms would boast similarly heavyweight line-ups. One critic in no doubt as to who should win, however, was Mikhail Bakhtin. "The novel is the sole genre that continues to develop, that is at yet uncompleted," he writes in *The Dialogic Imagination*; "it alone is organically receptive to new forms of mute perception." Poor old epic poetry, allowed to come up with the idea for Joyce's *Ulysses* but forbidden from expressing it for itself. Yet contemporary poetry is full of retold epics in one form or another, from Christopher Logue's *War Music* to Ciaran Carson's *The Táin* and Alice Oswald's *Memorial* – a list to which Daljit Nagra has now added his retelling of the *Ramayana*.

An epic is a "poem containing history", thought Ezra Pound, and the *Ramayana* has more history than most: the earliest written version is 2,000 years old. Pound's baggy epic largely bypasses India, but Yeats knew the *Ramayana*, and takes from it the female character of his early poem

'Anashuya and Vijaya'. Yeats's love of India came with a heavy dose of Orientalist fantasy, as when he announced that democracy in that country would "destroy... the caste system that has saved Indian intellect". Nagra's retelling of the tale makes a poor defence witness for the caste system. On the most basic levels of diction and narration, this is a self-consciously mongrelised text, solemn one moment, cartoonish the next, high-flown, demotic, majestic and chaotic all at once. The various languages of India have contributed numerous words to the English language, including such Kipling-era slang as 'chokey', 'pukka', 'buckshee', 'wallah' and 'doolally', and when Nagra wants to sound colloquial he affects a strangely old-time or mock-tabloid style, as though about to break into a barrack-room ballad or versify a *Sun* headline. For an updated text, the language feels weirdly dated: the weapons of the gods are "snazzy", Rama is so strong he can "heave-ho" a cliff; feasting is "pearly-teeth drollery", expressions of surprise are school of Grampa Simpson ("by jiminy"), grief is feeling "boo-hooey", and an attractive woman displays "hot-babe-ness". The linguistic exuberance often seems too knowingly 'vibrant', to use that term so awkwardly applied by the culture industry to any multicultural activity. It is seen to best effect in passages that might be described (another nod to Bakhtin) as carnivalesque, as in this description of Raavana's court:

> In terms of teeth, the ladies varnish
> their teeth black as sapphire or egg-plant purple,
> who but holy-molies have stained-white dentures!
>
> Worst of all for Vishnu well-wishers –
> ample boozy brain-idle womankind
> are snogging stubbly men or baldly kissing fellow ladies.

A few pages further on and a woman is a "Curvaceous succulent beautification's copper-hair-tossing / mesmeric damsel", possessed of "bounteous yet conically chiselled chest-smackers!" I can only imagine the Gordian knot of mock-heroic hyperbole from which Nagra has extracted this overwrought and frankly cringe-worthy construction. For a more sober Nagra, compare the section in which Rama laments the loss of Sita, and his subsequent quest to track her down, even if the section in question is called "You Hot Monkey!"

Arshia Sattar, the translator of the Penguin *Ramayana*, has written of wincing at translations of ancient epics "littered with 'thees', 'thous', 'wherefores', and 'it would behove you, sire' even though these translations were produced at a time long after such words and phrases fell out of common usage". This is not to say that archaism does not have its place in translating epic, when used as a marker of comic anachronism (think of the Cyclops chapter in *Ulysses*). The slang doesn't always ring true, either: "larrikins" are people for instance, not antics, as Nagra seems to think. At its best, the wrong-note effect of Nagra's translationese ennobles rather than infantilises, and reminds us of the out-of-jointness of epic form in the lyric foothills that make up most contemporary poetry.

Bakhtin worried about "mute perception", by which I presume he meant the shortage of characters in ancient epics who read the newspapers or watch TV. Yet Nagra's text is full of mute perceptions for the reader, or rather typographical signs of the text battling to reconnect with the barbaric yawp of orality. I counted the letter 'm' 68 times in Vishnu's mantra ("om"), and when things get violent the words "stomachs", "spleens", "giblets", "blood water" and "gore galore" bring the type out in a rash more usually associated with children's party invitations. When in doubt change font, it would seem. Also noteworthy is Nagra's continuing love affair with the exclamation mark. You'd think one was enough for most emotions, but frequently Nagra insists on not one but three!!! They have their joco-serious uses, but enough is enough after a while, and one is reminded of Adorno's comparison of the over-use of exclamation marks by the Expressionists to the multiple zeroes of Weimar Republic banknotes; hyperinflation is not the most sound basis for a poetic economy either, and it is to be hoped that Nagra can find some way of bringing his exclamatory form of the German 'zero stroke' under control.

As for the plot: Rama and Bharat vie for the kingship; Rama, Lakshmana and Sita go walkabout and have a run-in with the temptress Soorpanaka; Sugreeva and Bali do battle for the throne of the monkey kingdom and... it doesn't make sense, exactly, to talk of 'spoilers' for a story already several thousand years old, but Nagra's text is more than proof against the banality of paraphrase. Suffice to say it all ends with a bang. The celebrations of the monkey army gathered to attack Sita's abductors nicely synthesises the sublime and the ridiculous, but once the battle proper starts I was reminded of watching a *Lord of the Rings* film and realising that the last hour had consisted mainly of the word "ouch" in Orc language: "All roared / Yaaaaaaaaaaaah! // Or roared Huzzaaaaaaaaaah!

// Above all / haaalaaahaaalaaaaaaaaaaaa" (sorry, I can't reproduce the funny fonts here). With a closing comic touch, Nagra ends with the words "Shanti! Shanti! Shanti!" In the waste land of contemporary epic poems in translation, Nagra has coaxed an improbable flower vividly, if rather too garishly, into bloom.

Aingeal Clare has written for the Guardian, TLS *and* London Review of Books.

COTTAGE INK

Moniza Alvi, At the Time of Partition, *Bloodaxe*, £9.95
ISBN 9781852249847
Maitreyabandhu, The Crumb Road, *Bloodaxe*, £9.95
ISBN 9781852249748

reviewed by Matthew Jarvis

. . .

Moniza Alvi's *At the Time of Partition* sent me outwards from the book itself to read more widely about the event at its heart – the 1947 partition of the British Indian empire that created the independent states of India and Pakistan. I mention this reaction simply because it encapsulates the fact that, whatever my reservations, this volume of poetry engaged my attention deeply, driving me right into the complex history out of which it emerges.

At the Time of Partition is a single narrative poem, divided into 20 parts – chapters, if you wish to see this as a verse novel. Alvi's tale is rooted in family stories, imagining the turbulent relocation of her grandmother's family from their home in Ludhiana (in what became independent India) to Lahore (in what became Pakistan). Bound up with this, as a central strand of the narrative, is the fate of Athar, one of the family's three sons, who is described in part one ('The Line') as "the young man with the damaged mind". Athar, brain-damaged after being hit by a lorry as a boy, is lost in the chaos of relocation and his absence is one of the key wounds of the text – alongside the loss of home and the struggles of reforming identity. Indeed, for this reader, Alvi's rendition of her grandmother's unsuccessful search for Athar, who had been entrusted to "friends of friends" for the journey to Lahore, was both profoundly moving and admirably well achieved: "She'd glimpse his face // from a great height, / from alongside, from underneath, // find him squatting / at the back of a textile factory. // In an instant, he'd be gone." Here, Alvi's relatively simple linguistic register – rendered, however, in well-worked structures of parallelism and with a shrewd use of contrasting sentence-length – crucially keeps the reins on the situation's emotion and the consequent impact is all the greater for it.

However, notwithstanding such observations, it was actually language that gave me some pause here. Of course, there is manifest linguistic skill. For example, the spiralling of rumour and fear as the family faces leaving home is handled with an accomplished building of linguistic pressure ("And the rumour of a rumour // And the acting on a rumour // And the kernel of a rumour"). But at other times, language becomes a little flat. Thus, the description of Lahore's demographic changes, the way it had to "contend with the mass departure / of its Hindus and Sikhs" and "cope with the influx / of a million Muslim refugees", sounds to me rather too like a textbook. In related fashion, "The rawness of her loss" comes perilously close to cliché, as does the description of people's sense that, although they had survived, "whole chunks were missing". It is as though, in the telling of such a compelling tale, the poetic eye occasionally slips away from its linguistic medium. Nonetheless, I can't get away from the fact that *At the Time of Partition* drew in my attention inexorably, even if I felt its language was sometimes lacking. I suspect this is a book I will keep coming back to.

The Crumb Road, by Maitreyabandhu (born Ian Johnson, but writing under the name he was given when he was "ordained into the Triratna Buddhist Order", as the book's biographical note helpfully explains), is another volume that drew me successfully into the orbit of its concerns. I particularly enjoyed the poems of childhood in the first of its three sections. 'Burial', for example, recalls an incident in which the speaker's father, "digging below the lilac trees", finds human bones, skulls, and with them a "stench" which "clambered through his chest, / then through his head". However, the subtlety of the poem is in the speaker's sudden realisation that something "isn't right": "I've made it up or rather I've mistaken / my father's story for the thing itself". Recollection proves unreliable, as the poem's vibrant details are revealed to be ungrounded in the speaker's actual experience. Another childhood poem is 'Bottle Digging', which is a fine evocation of complex father-son relationships. Here, engaging in his father's past-time of digging for bottles – but conscious of how, as a young boy, he "didn't have the heart much less the strength" to dig as well as his father did – the speaker recalls a moment of triumph when he finds a "cottage ink" (an ink bottle shaped like a cottage). However, in his innocence – and as his father watches on, unspeaking – he is persuaded by a collector to exchange this rarity for three other bottles that are far less precious. As the speaker's younger self is confronted by his father's subsequent open acknowledgement of how the boy has "been duped", the poem concludes with the striking declaration that "I'm still ashamed of what I did".

The second section of the volume is perhaps most clearly defined by work which seems notably spiritual or philosophical in its concerns. Thus, 'Rangiatea' responds to the Māori mythical space of the poem's title, whilst 'Letters on Cézanne' suggests nothing less than a philosophy of being. In this latter piece, then, the notion of colours "in a / perpetual dialogue and exchange" draws the poet to the conclusion that "It should be the same with us: / the Yes balancing out the No, Joy calming Despair / without cancellation: a day of sun and a day of rain". Significantly, there is no sense in which revelation is tacked onto the end of the poem simply to provide a rhetorically resonant conclusion; rather, the finish here is the explicit outworking of ideas that are pursued through the rest of the piece. However, it is childhood and youth that again dominate the third section of the book, in an extended sequence, 'Stephen', that looks back to a formative but secret relationship between two boys. As in the rest of the volume, much of the power of Maitreyabandhu's writing is in the understated nature of its expression: thus, even at the moment of tragedy, when Stephen is killed by a car, the description remains quiet ("he'd been waiting to do something with his life / when someone screamed as a woman we both knew / turned right and knocked him off his bike"). *The Crumb Road* is, I think, a fine example of how potent a poetry of quiet expression can be.

Matthew Jarvis is the Anthony Dyson Fellow in Poetry at the University of Wales Trinity Saint David.

INJUSTICE SHE HAS WITNESSED

Eavan Boland, New Selected Poems, *Carcanet*, £14.95
ISBN 9781847772411
Lorna Goodison, Oracabessa, *Carcanet*, £12.95
ISBN 9781847772428

reviewed by Sophie Mayer

. . .

'The Emigrant Irish' was the first Eavan Boland poem I encountered, as a Poem on the Underground in 1994. Citing the "dread, makeshift example" of Irish immigrants fleeing the Great Famine, the poem placed the British colonial legacy in the heart of London's transport system. Since *The Journey*, Boland's work has kept that legacy in focus and in motion. As her prior collection from 2007 was entitled, the relation between England and Ireland is one of *Domestic Violence*, not least for Boland, who spent part of her childhood in England and who writes in English.

The title of the final poem in this *New Selected*, 'A Woman Without a Country', represents that dispossession, but also a longing for belonging: the title refers to Virginia Woolf's assertion "As a woman, I have no country", but rather than Woolf's contestatory pride, the poem is full of mourning in its observation of engraving "a bony line forever / severing / Her body from its native air". That violence and grief are at once gendered and colonial; poems across Boland's career, such as 'The Achill Woman', 'The Dolls Museum in Dublin' and 'In Which Hester Bateman, Eighteenth-Century English Silversmith, Takes an Irish Commission', make complex play with both the lived histories of women, and with the *aisling*, the female dream-figure of Éire who appears in the dreams of male bards.

Boland transposes the *aisling* through two figures from Graeco-Roman mythology: Daphne, figure for the former colony paralysed by the assault of the colonial power, and Persephone, a figure for the hellish experiences of colonialism. Daphne, in parallel, stands for the impossibility of the woman poet, contrasted with Persephone/Demeter, of whom Boland writes in 'The Pomegranate':

> The only legend I have ever loved is
> the story of a daughter lost in hell.
> And found and rescued there.
>
> [...]
>
> And the best thing about the legend is
> I can enter it anywhere. And have.

Rather than the frozen "Daphne with her thighs in bark", whom, in the poem of that title, the speaker brusquely advises to 'Rut with him' [Apollo], the twinned Persephone/Demeter offers mobile points of identification. Interconnected with Boland's concern with the silencing of both Irish and women's voices is the valence of motherhood as a site from which to stage a challenge. 'Mother Ireland' brings the two tropes together, ending with the Demeter-like invocation, "*Come back to us* / they said. / *Trust me* I whispered".

Among the new poems that end the *Selected* is 'Becoming Anne Bradstreet', who famously addressed her first collection as "Thou ill-formed offspring of my feeble brain". While Boland is less maternal towards her work, engraving is not the only ambivalent metaphor used for putting the self on the page. In 'Suburban Woman: V', the poet addresses her poetic self:

> Defeated we survive, we two, housed
>
> together in my compromise, my craft.
> Who are of one another the first draft.

'A Woman Painted on a Leaf', the final poem in her 1995 *Collected*, is included here, with its bitter, shocking final lines "Let me. // Let me die."

As Anne Fogarty has observed, Boland's work has "become increasingly spare and honed", both in moving from Yeatsian stanzas to free verse and even free mise-en-page (as in 'Mother Ireland', which presents a contoured river or coastline through its indents), and also in the lasering-in of attention to the seemingly irreducible and unresolvable conflicts of writing from a place of erasure. This is intensified by Boland's shift to the use of sequences: iterations (to pick up on Boland's interest in coding) trying to resolve the impossible equation. Lorna Goodison's *Oracabessa* is likewise composed of sequences, but the poems interrelate more in the manner of "Miles Marley Mozart" ('From the Bard's Book of Common Prayer'). Complex musical structures underpin the collection's constant criss-cross movement: from the Caribbean to North America to Europe and back, and across all the languages, dialects, cultures and faiths of three continents, reconfiguring the Triangle Trade and its deep scars:

An injustice she has witnessed: the loveliest
of earth's yield laid claim to by the privileged;
this being a form of hoarding.

Medicine is Miles Marley Mozart taken in the air.

Oracabessa – goldenhead – is concerned exactly with raw materials, their imperialist corruption and the possibility of cure: black and gold are held in tension. The collection opens with 'To Make Various Kinds of Black', a meditation on Cennini's instructions to painters, which contrasts "Black of scorched earth, of torched stones of peach; / twisted trees that bore strange fruit" with other shades of black that, made of soot, are available to all. Black, Goodison unpacks, is "just perfect as it is", inverting the alchemical suggestion of the collection's title.

Goodison's work is exactly metaphysical, concerned with transmutations. She says of Donne that trying to understand his conceits "worked free // the bound roots of my within" after her father's death ('Reading Through the Walls'). Like Boland, Goodison re-visions canonical poetry, predominantly white and male, "as hints for her own journey … [but] disoriented" ('Quest') by its mash-up with blues, Danny Kaye, *Gitanjali* and "a rizzla-rolled spliff" ('Need'). In 'From the Bard's Book…' Goodison sets out her manifesto for "the commonwealth of the written word", critical of another form of hoarding: a story that Robert Southey "snapped shut the book he was reading" when visitors arrived "as if... what was printed / therein had been set down for his eyes alone".

Instead, *Oracabessa* is an open reading of *Omeros*, the magnum opus of the collection's dedicatee, Derek Walcott. In its more diffuse form, it gently questions the drive of the epic, its debt to heroic narratives, and simultaneously unfolds the spiritual charge of seeking, asking (in 'Bookmarks for Eyes', whose title at once rewords Shakespeare and suggests the potentially blinding effect of textual culture):

> What am I searching for outside this known
> world, why am I a followfashion Columbus
> gone off the map, and here there be dragons.

Instead, Goodison opens her book and operates as a reverse Columbus, tracing lyric back to Al-Andalus in 'Not Sadness', where Song and God mingle beings. Goodison's lyric is reminiscent of the "epic lyric" Dean Rader observes in contemporary Native American poetry, in which vast scope, scape and scale are traversed in compact forms, framed by a precise, grounded and joyous spirituality.

"Channelling through the Holy Ghost sistren. / Sistren who is a sireen, a love siren", Goodison is an exuberant envoy from a "small island", similar to Boland's, where colonial legacies, including gendered silences, continue to shape speech ('I Am a Love Siren'). Through the tripping half-rhymed triplets of 'Remember Us in Motherland', the poet names herself "chantwelle", kin to griots, sangomas and Usain Bolt. "Marked by Africa", she writes from what Paul Gilroy calls a diasporic "cosmopolitanism". Boland's words for Anne Bradstreet could apply to both poets: "We say *home truths* / Because her words can be at home anywhere – ". Poets on and of the underground of history and myth, of nation and gender, they are Orphic singers: Boland mourning her daughter/country/voice lost and found, while Goodison finds a complex joy in her quest to "reorient her heart" toward Heartease ('Not Sadness').

Sophie Mayer's publications include The Private Parts of Girls *(Salt, 2011).*

BUSY INSIDE THE SCENERY

Rachael Boast, Pilgrim's Flower, *Picador, £9.99*
ISBN 9781447242178
David Morley, The Gypsy and the Poet, *Carcanet, £9.95*
ISBN 9781847771247
Helen Mort, Division Street, *Chatto & Windus, £12*
ISBN 9780701186845

reviewed by Joey Connolly

. . .

From the off, Rachael Boast's *Pilgrim's Flower* does not shy from wearing its referentiality on its sleeve: the opening words of the collection are "Resembling Cocteau, the two statues in the pillars / of the fireplace have been busy inside the scenery" – the book's first act is to call on something absent from itself. The poem, 'The Place of Five Secrets', gradually reveals itself to derive from Cocteau's *La Belle et la Bête* and the poem struggles, almost visibly, to define itself as independent of the film. The observations are sharp, the attention to detail a pleasure: "the five secrets / of Bête who is not himself, even on a good day" is so much better for its lack of a comma after 'Bête', which creates an object 'Bête-who-is-not-himself', rather than 'Bête', who happens not to be himself. But there's an undefined portentousness or grandiosity which threatens to overshadow the emotional tenor of the poem. Ending with *"ne faut pas regarder / dans mes yeux* turned around by key, mirror, / horse, glove, and the rose at the centre of it all" demonstrates just this kind of overdriven minting of poignancy, without holding in mind very much to be poignant about.

Several pages of endnotes contribute to an impression that significant action might be taking place offstage; there is information which is considered important enough to include in the book, but is somehow not appropriate for the actual poem itself. This trick can be productive: think of Eliot's winky 'explanation' of *The Waste Land*, or the infinite proliferation of data implied by the notes-within-notes of David Foster Wallace. But Boast is too reliant on atmospherics for these poems to bear being tugged apart like this, and – even when there's no note provided – it feels all too often as if something crucial to the enjoyment of the poem isn't included in the words on the page. The attention is being constantly directed outwards, *from* the poem itself and *toward* the endnotes. When the notes read "See Cocteau's poem *'L'ange Heurtebise'*", we're led even further outwards.

This centrifugal force away from the centres of these poems works oddly alongside the gravity evoked by Boast's formal and idiomatic choices (one poem is in perfect Sapphic syllabics; others reappropriate a Cocteau film, or Akhmatova's diary, or the myth of Marsyas). The poems haul in so much cultural and literary baggage, an alternative metaphor might see each poem acting as some kind of transport hub, in which the variegated roar of well-dressed crowds rushing inwards and outwards leaves very little attention spare to be paid to the architecture of the station itself. And all-too-often the architecture is a little too generic, a little too insubstantial as anything but a channel for the flow of reference. When Boast makes this weaving into and out of reference part of her subject, as in the excellent is-she-isn't-she biblical allusion of 'The Scribe's Migraine', the poems are clever and affecting. And there are several poems here which avoid the danger of referentiality – the sequences, which do build their own worlds, tend to be mesmeric and moving – but the book is all too often dogged by this essential problem.

The endnotes in David Morley's *The Gypsy and the Poet* work very differently to Boast's. Morley's notes don't reach into his poems; they exist in order to situate them as self-sufficient objects in the world. One informs us of the location in which certain poems were written, and another that some of the poems are painted onto bird boxes now attached to trees. So that, Morley notes, the "birds nested in a poem about themselves". This beautiful conception of the poems captures something central to the collection; that is, the preoccupation here with the relationship between language and the natural world as somehow formative of, and inhabiting, each other.

It is the conceit of Morley's collection which allows him to approach such a potentially tired topic (to match the unappealing title) in an inventive way. The book's main body comprises two sonnet sequences describing the real-world relationship between John Clare and a gypsy, Wisdom Smith. Although there are moments when the poet/gypsy dichotomy pushes Morley towards a slightly over-conventional binary distinction between the two – poet attuned only to the reductive romance of nature; gypsy as earthy possessor of the "Deepest / of the Deep" – for most of the time, it evolves a complex and involving relationship between language, social position and nature.

In 'The Ditch', the natural world is voiced – as the thoughts of frogs – in italics: "*The poet's coat and hat*, they thought, *were rain clouds. / The scribbling pen and riffling paper: they were the rain. / The cloud and rain have moved like lovers out of sight.*" Later, outside italics, we get "the lovers and rain move like clouds out of sight; / a scribbling paper and riffling rain: they are the pen"; this is a poetry in which nature and language cycle down through one another. Each is productive, in turn, of the other. It's not only a profound piece of criticism of Clare's work, but also an intriguing statement on the ways we understand – and impute voice to – nature. As the things of the natural word move through each other, so language moves down through Clare, to Morley, to ourselves.

This effect is heightened throughout by a dazed swaying in and out of rhyme: patterned end-rhyme dissolves unpredictably into thick internal-rhyme and assonantal music. Continuing throughout the sonnet sequence, this effect adds further to the impression that synthetic forms cannot hold against the anarchic spontaneity of the natural world being described. The organised human world is run up against the wilderness again in a fine version of Lorca's poem 'Reyerta', from his *Gypsy Ballads*, where Morley gives us the stunning "microcircuitry of cicadas": a complete departure from Lorca, and the more wonderful for it. The implication is that the language we each, personally, bring to our perceptions interacts with our understanding of the world.

In *The Gypsy and the Poet*, Morley has taken a situation, and a set of concepts and limitations, and has made repeated use of them in a resolute and insightful way. The result is a valuably original writing of nature, and a valuable collection of poetry.

From its confrontational cover image to the "striking miners" of the blurb, to the jacket's daubish font and its endorsement by Michael Symmons Roberts evoking "the bedrock of the north of England", everything seems determined to sell Helen Mort's *Division Street* as being about Sheffield, the North, industrial decline. But it isn't. To insist that she is writing about the North is to mistake setting for subject.

Mort's central sequence 'Scab' is a case in point. Opening with a scatter of glib biblical analogies – "the wine / turning to water in the pubs, / the tax man ransacking the Church, / plenty of room at every inn" – which take the place of any serious engagement with industrial communities in Northern England in the 1980s, it soon becomes clear that some hazy parallel is being drawn – intentionally or not – between the struggle of the miners and Mort's own struggle to acclimatise to her time at Cambridge University, to handle "a wine / everyone else is able to pronounce". It is, in the face of the deprivation and communal devastation to which Mort alludes, somewhat difficult to sympathise with the Cambridge student anxiously reconstructing ("This is a reconstruction", the poem points out, twice) the struggles of the 1980s industrial North as an analogy of class struggle amid the "fish-tail ballgowns" and "free champagne" of Cambridge. It's astonishing, in fact, that Mort can satirise the impulse to "make a blockbuster / from this", while making an equivalent poetic gesture herself.

If we're willing to forget about the claim to talk about the North, though, the "division" of the title can take on a different meaning. Mort is far stronger when writing about pitfalls and misdirections in the project of knowing oneself. There's an eerie portrait of 'The Girl Next Door', who stands "in her kitchen, head tipped back, the way I stand"; and in a translation from Piranesi, we might note the glimpse of "a man / much like my father" – an unsettling phrase, given that fathers in poems are always, at best, only 'much like'. This thematic concern shows Mort to possess a sure-handed and intelligent way with words.

All the more puzzling and frustrating, then, that so many poems here bluff out into contrived wordplay just at the moment where something real might happen. In 'End':

coming
is *le petit mort.*

I understand.
I've died already

at your hand.

The po-faced pseudo-significance is as far from erotic as anything I can image. Similarly catastrophic is "*What links the fire of London and the colour blue? / I'm wondering if a match would be enough / or if there's really no smoke without you.*" This is, too frequently, a poetry of the easy option – an obscurantist punnery taking the place of any deep engagement.

In the same way, then, Division Street – as the actual street – doesn't get much of a look in. Rather, it's there as its two words: as a snappy title, suggestive of the break-up described in the poem. And, disappointingly, this sleight of hand – the cheap trick switched into the place we might expect something real or profound – seems to be the characteristic move in *Division Street.*

Joey Connolly received an Eric Gregory Award in 2012.

EARTH'S HOLDINGS

Philip Gross, Later, *Bloodaxe, £9.95*
ISBN 9781852249793
Jean Sprackland, Sleeping Keys, *Cape, £10*
ISBN 9780224097697
Chris Jones, Jigs and Reels, *Shoestring, £6*
ISBN 9781907356681

reviewed by Carol Rumens

. . .

If Memory is the mother of the Muses, Time must be their grandmother. Poetry is particularly conscious of the ancestral connection. It holds onto memory partly by manipulating rhythm, slowing the passage of time while revealing its sneaky irreversible movements. Poetry can go anywhere, but clings to its time-honoured subjects, still: the changing seasons, the vagaries of love, the death of loved ones, the need to seize the day. If time, for most writers, no longer includes the grand dimension of post mortem eternity, that loss has made it all the more pressing a subject, and boosted the elegy to its place as genre-in-chief in contemporary poetry.

Later is a magnificent extended elegy, formally adventurous, poised between narrative and metaphysics, themes and variation. The epigraph quotes Michael Wood's introduction to Edward Said's *On Late Style*. "Dead persons have certainly got themselves beyond time," Wood writes, "but then what temporal longing lurks in our calling them 'late'?" I've always understood 'late' in this pronominal sense simply to abbreviate a phrase too full-blown for modern taste – 'late-lamented'. The need to mourn aloud for the recently (lately) dead also 'lurks' in the term, and many of Gross's poems are concerned with the final illness and death of his Estonian father, John Karl Gross, in 2011. But they are not simply laments and death-narratives, being interleaved with a life-story about a young man crossing borders and changing countries, moving in geographical space as well as time.

In 'Home, 1990' the refugee-parent resists his chance to go back with a poignant question (*"What could I do // by going... except see / it was gone?"*) while, on the facing page, his identity merges with the iconic figures in the 'Stroke Ward', "sunk now / in some strait between mealtime / and myth..." Everything is process, and none of these poems is content with stillness. The stepped, irregular, spreading forms of Gross's late style ensure moments of searching and doubt are part of the texture. Even in a more traditional structure like the 'Glosa: Westron Wynde', the poem closest to pure lament, the search for the right word is part of the subject, "The wind / still held its... not quite a note, / rather, a space into which a note might go..."

Among the more exploratory poems in the book (and there is an impressive cohort), 'Closed Loops' makes ingenious use of anaphora to devise a complex and combative prose-poem form. The speaker, watching as the sick man, haunted by strange "nightcomers", begins to lose his grip on words, grapples fiercely to batten them in "closed loops" and iron hoops of syntax. Simultaneously, there's a desperation to escape "the judgement of the heart" which "Beats on. The sentence: life, life, life." This is a painful, emphatic and clotted poem. Mostly, the textures are lighter, and the metaphysics evolved is not about closure at all, but the onward flow of existence. Individuals are "a resting place, a night stop" in the beautiful poem 'Legacy'. Biology makes light of time in the image of birds migrating "through / that space called *me* at one time, // at another, *you* or *you*". Like the human concept of identity, poetry's tight-folded lyric is careful opened out in *Later*. The stepping and spacing give the lines time to think aloud as they travel across and down the page, and over the edges of the pages.

In Jean Sprackland's *Sleeping Keys*, the house controls the itinerary of volatile substances – water, electricity, time itself. The overarching metaphor holds these poems of divorce and new love in a lyric-narrative blend which is both condensed and outward-looking. There are stories within stories and houses within houses in this ingenious building. In 'Homemaking', for example, the act of slicing bread reminds the speaker of a dilapidated zoo she once lived near, where cages each contain "a loaf of bread and a family of mice". The mice eat the bread and sleep in the tunnels they've hollowed out until nothing's left. It's a parable of doomed survival, yet almost charmingly comic until the closing memory of "that ruined street of bread houses, / their desperate smell under the high-watt bulbs".

Sprackland, like Gross, is an avid word-collector and brings the inner workings of her houses to physical life with special vocabularies, "naming the parts: / *swan neck, hopper head, anglepiece, shoe*" ('The Covenant'). But the poet of house-time knows the pathos of concrete is that it doesn't remain concrete. The book's epigraph is from *To The Lighthouse*: "One feather and the house, sinking, falling, would have turned and pitched downwards to the depths of darkness." Sprackland puts it less fancifully than Woolf: "Earth's holdings are mud, and all our buildings / are straws drawing up water" ('Footings'). Houses can be rebuilt, of course, and dead objects may only be sleeping, as in the title poem. Giving off a "flinty scent" from their biscuit-tin, the redundant keys could be dangerous "treasure" and must be binned, now the spaces they opened are only memories – slightly clichéd erotic ones, in this instance.

These poems are not chronologically late (Sprackland, b.1962, is a decade younger than Gross) but they balance the panache and energy of middle-age ("This new love is a tall place to live") with the awareness of mortality bequeathed by the death of parents. Sprackland's elegy for her mother, 'Last Resort', is a superb four-part narrative which makes space for the anecdotes she does so memorably, beginning with the finding of a new antibiotic by a young missionary in the Borneo jungle, and including an encounter in a hospital lift with a falconer and his hawk. A 'letters home' sequence threaded through the collection is not always so sharply distinct from the dominant voice as to qualify as a sub-plot, though it includes some gems, like the odd, anguished little war-poem in which the "*rain has a different sound: / water touching water, // the ecstatic meeting / of like with like, / itself a homecoming.*"

Chris Jones's *Jigs and Reels* comes from an oral tradition which includes the broadside ballad and performance poetry. But his are literary in ambition, too, and designed for the page. They form the middle section of this short book, and all have paired titles and eight quatrains, divided between facing pages into two sets of four. Four-beat lines move at a strongly marked pace, and combine a swashbuckling, carefree tone with moments of sharp description, as when the speaker in 'Bristle/Blemish' studies his baby's hair "for rufous, auburn, curls turned fair, / the brown then red tinge of his lashes, / this pinch of fur around his ears / and copper brows as fine as foxes."

Jones's ballad-like form is surprisingly adaptable: there are elegies which share the freewheeling style but, thanks to the rhythmic urgency, seem no less heart-felt. Most of this collection would no doubt sound attractive in performance. On the page, though, the rhyming often seems hit-or-miss, with an amateurish habit of pairing singular and plural rhyme-words. Recollecting a meeting with Thom Gunn in 'An Invitation'("Thom shows me round his airy home / of lacquered timbers banked with tomes...") Jones reveals the extent of his aspiration, and that he still has skills to learn from the "streetwise dude(s)" (Gunn himself, Tony Harrison, Ken Smith) who are his mentors.

Carol Rumens's most recent collection is De Chirico's Threads *(Seren, 2010).*

DREAM TESTICLES AND MEMPHIS GUILT

Mark Strand, Almost Invisible, *Waywiser, £8.99*
ISBN 9781904130567
Don Share, Union, *Eyewear, £12.99*
ISBN 9781908998101

reviewed by Ben Wilkinson

. . .

Mark Strand cuts a longstanding figure in post-war American poetry, somewhere between its ageing Buddy Holly and its benign – if somewhat sinister – grandfather. His first books, published in the late 60s, marked him out as a connoisseur of concision, approaching stock themes of absence and negation through a blend of realism and surrealist imagery, and a dark humour that steered feeling clear of sentiment. Since then, his poetry has continued to mine that metaphysical seam, though the early dash and vigour have eased, as if our poet had mellowed with age. All of which wouldn't be a problem, if the poetry hadn't also gradually slackened. *Almost Invisible*, Strand's thirteenth collection and one that consists entirely of riddling prose poems (the man himself won't deign to give them *that* dubious classification, though it's really the only halfway useful one), is, if nothing else, evidence of the teetering line between good and bad poetry. Every poem's success hangs in a fine linguistic balancing act: a fact that poets forget at their peril.

The book opens promisingly enough. 'A Banker in the Brothel of Blind Women' is a parable of sorts, telling the tale of a deceived and deceiving suit who poses as a shepherd:

> "My dear," said the banker to the same woman, "I can tell that you are a rich widow looking for a little excitement and are not blind at all." "This observation suggests," said the woman, "that you may be a shepherd after all, for what kind of rich widow would find excitement being a whore only to end up with a banker?" "Exactly," said the banker.

Extending Strand's time-honoured obsession with selfhood and the social masks we wear, this piece offsets philosophical solemnity with a dry and ready wit. Identity's hall of mirrors is not dissimilarly dissected in 'Harmony in the Boudoir', a comic foray into intimacy that sees a man pompously declaring his unknowable "true self" to his partner. That he is brilliantly described doing so while "kicking off his slippers", only to find his beloved gently mocking his overblown confessions, is a comic masterstroke, not to mention tonally spot on. "Oh you silly man," taunts his wife: "That you barely exist as you are couldn't please me more."

Sadly, most of the rest of *Almost Invisible* is far from pitch-perfect. So far, in fact, you half suspect its obviously gifted author must be playing tone deaf. Things take a decisive turn for the worse with the tritely mystical 'The Students of the Ineffable', 13 lines of hollow prose that, for me, are more than effable, but we'll keep this above the belt. Which is more than can be said for Strand: 'Dream Testicles, Vanished Vaginas', a squib every bit as bad as its title implies, is worse still. Fantasy it may be, but you surely have to suspend more than disbelief to think of genitals as "open, honest, and energetic". Or, better yet, "forthright and gifted". The portentous tone may disguise the fact it's obviously a joke, but either way it's an exceptionally weak one, and represents a low point in the kind of lazy surrealism that's been exported and – regrettably – far-too-readily embraced on this side of the Atlantic. A sickly blend of faux naivety and smug knowingness, it's the tacked-on mock profundity that rankles most, one the reader knows as well as the poet is nothing but an emotional and intellectual cul-de-sac. Or maybe it's just the thought of "testicles... swinging dreamily among the clouds like little chandeliers" that makes you want to reach for your gun.

That said, *Almost Invisible* is not without occasional charm. A handful of lapidary gems surface: the desperation and willed detachment evoked by 'Clear in the September Light'; the haunting dream-world conjured by 'The Mysterious Arrival of an Unusual Letter'; the misguided wishful-thinking of 'Once Upon a Cold November Morning'. But much here is no more than bogusly gnomic and flippantly inconsequential stuff; so much so you begin to wish, unkindly, that Strand had more often kept in mind the title of one particular poem: 'An Event About Which No More Need Be Said'. Applying such wisdom to many of the alternately windy, and irritating musings collected here would surely have made *Almost Invisible* a better book – or, failing that, a shorter one. The poem in question? Something about a mysterious prince showing off his malformed penis in the back of a cab. Taxi!

Don Share is best known on these shores as the editor of *Poetry*, a US monthly and the English-speaking world's leading poetry magazine – excepting possibly the present publication, of course. On the back cover of his first collection, *Union*, which Eyewear Publishing has cannily republished as an introduction to Share's work for us Brits, he grins from his author mugshot as if he didn't receive more poetry-as-electronic-gunk jamming his inbox each day than any other person on the planet, and all credit to him for it. If *Union* is anything to go by, for Share, life and poetry aspire to be guided by our most generous instincts – or at least should. His often single-stanza, rhythmically dexterous narrative poems delight in the particularities, peculiarities and cultural loam of modern life – childhood is remembered as "condensed milk, the family Bible, / savings passbooks, Nero Wolfe and Mickey Spillane paperbacks" – while also striving to make sense of it, in the context of histories both personal and public. In the same poem, 'Signals Over Hill', the speaker reflects how "roots are, themselves, a form of rootlessness".

It's an idea that directs much of this earthy, hard-thinking, undeceived yet hopeful book, from poems that tell of personal grief and marital separation such as 'Sweet Life', a lament for the "self-love" that promises false happiness in "any place we never lived", to those that plumb the depths of the American Civil War, and the former slave state of Tennessee where Share grew up. "We fought America in ourselves," declares 'Dilemma', echoing the title poem's fractured blues song: "Memphis was born / from abolished ruins // Memphis forgot / that Memphis is guilt". Pitched against this is a kind of spiritual faith, a cautious belief in meliorism, and a sense of absolute unity to be had in commune with the natural world. You can forgive the occasionally affected and anachronistic tone of piety in certain pieces, if only for the very genuine way Share recognises, and evokes the fact, that pain is always part of our contentment:

> So summer's last leaves blow
> banded in the paling sunlight,
> and as the weather turns just now
> too cool to stay outside,
>
> all our affairs soften
> into the collected past,
> the honey all gone
> from hives closed by winter's reach
>
> *and I reject happiness in order,*
> *precisely in order, to remember it.*

Though portentousness may occasionally get the better of it, *Union* is a big-hearted and reassuringly human collection of poems, and one that's not without humour. I'd certainly take it over much of the arch clever-clever masquerading as poetry that's out there just now. Like the portrait of his father-in-law in 'Spiritual', the kind of man who "always shook you by the hand / and gave you every drop of wisdom he ever had", it suggests Share as the sort of poet of which we can sometimes seem in short supply.

Ben Wilkinson reviews for the Guardian and TLS. His poems were shortlisted for the inaugural Picador Poetry Prize.

THE HUG MACHINE

Anne Carson, Red Doc>, *Cape, £12*
ISBN 978-0224097574

reviewed by Nuar Alsadir

. . .

how we
talk how we are allowed
to talk is

the most part of happy or
not

The above lines from Anne Carson's 'C' are placed in the mouth of
Lieutenant M'hek, a psychiatrist sent to help Sad, the latest incarnation
of Herakles from Carson's *Autobiography of Red*, based on Hercules's tenth
labour. Five seconds on Google will lead you to reviews contextualising
this novel in verse along with dutiful plot summary. Yet the most
compelling element of the work is the link between "how [Carson] /
talk[s]" how she has "allowed" herself to talk, and the sense that she has
figured out the secret to her "most part of happy".

There are many references to therapy in *Red Doc>*, particularly in
relation to the way one speaks – and, of course, whenever we speak we
are speaking to another person, real or imagined (or, in the case of a

therapist, real and imagined). Carson demonstrates this as we observe characters anticipating the response of others ("now you'll / say..."). Mikhail Bakhtin's theory of addressivity describes how anticipating the response of our addressee causes us to reshape our utterances, how we are apt to edit what we had intended to express so that it fits the reception we imagine, or project, onto our listener.

Who we speak to, in other words, shapes how we speak. The other character returning from *Autobiography of Red*, Geryon – here "G" – also yearns to talk in a certain way, to free associate, "simply say what comes to / mind to simply float." As *Red Doc>* continues the adventures of Sad and G, the most compelling approach is to let go of the narrative and its references, and keep your ear tuned to the "little zipper whine / that runs along the convolutes of [your] ear / licking in under every / bone like a bad emotion". A psychoanalyst attending to a patient on the couch may take a similar approach and listen, as W.R. Bion called for, with a suspension of memory, desire or understanding because the psychoanalyst, like the reader, "is seeking something that differs from what is normally known as reality". One, then, is attuned both to the story and to the affect accompanying the narrative elements – a less crude version of M'hek's not "car[ing] for people" but "what flows through them":

> His teacher at med
> school called him a
> minotaur who swallows
> other people's labyrinths.
> Good I'll do psychiatry he
> said.

We then turn the page to the next "poem" to learn that "[o]ther people's labyrinths really were tedious as it / turned out".

This insight can be applied to the characters in *Red Doc>* as well, which is perhaps why Carson does not bother to expand on their labyrinths, casting them as types and focusing instead on psychic flow. Visually, most of the poems are set in fixed margins, like a strip of labyrinth wall, holding what flows through like Temple Grandin's hug machine, meant to calm autistic children. Grandin's machine – inspired by the observation that cattle were visibly more serene when placed in a V-shaped squeeze-box during vaccinations – is a concrete example of what D.W. Winnicott called a "holding environment", a therapeutic recreation of the comfort a child feels when held by its mother. But why would the verse flowing across these pages need stanzaic hug boxes?

Perhaps similar to an addressee, a speaker, too, can be real or imagined – or, real and imagined. Through the character Ida, whose name, Carson writes, "is a verbal word for / the way / you see inside your mind", we learn that anxiety can be triggered by the thought of others witnessing your emotions. Ida is in therapy with the "CMO," "the Pig Doc" who, during a "session", responds to Ida's inquiry as to why she's always stealing, with "Because it's the opposite of feeling". He then continues his interpretation:

> To *feel* anything
> deranges you. To be seen
> *feeling* anything strips you
> naked...
> You think what
> will they do what new
> power will they acquire *if*
> *they see me naked like*
> *this.* If they see you
> *feeling.* You have no idea
> *what.* It's not about *them.*
> To be seen is the penalty.
> You shame victim after
> victim they are all *you.*

To have feelings is to be seen naked – to let observers ("*them*") have agency weakens you. Shaming others becomes a form of projective identification, defending against shameful feelings by splitting off bad feelings and projecting them into others (Carson's characters?), who then act out or express the feelings that have been disowned. At the close of the Pig Doc's interpretation, he seems to insist upon a reintegration of the split off parts into the self – "they are all *you*". The "*you*" in this poem is Ida, but if Ida's name means "the way you see into your mind", is *Red Doc>*, then, also Carson's drama of mind?

Posing that question – in fact, any thought of the author – feels like a violation of her way of talking rooted in a desire to uncover the real rather than what might be found when listening without memory, desire or understanding. Furthermore, an audience that acquires "new power" by seeing her in the act of feeling will likely alter the response she anticipates from her reader, recast her addressivity and, consequently, how she speaks – in short, queer the pitch.

To be fair to the reader, however, such an angle would likely be less tempting were the characters more satisfyingly fleshed-out. Interestingly, this is less the case when the characters are taken from literature, when the narrator is in the position of reader and we, the readers, *overread* much in the way Matthew Arnold described poetry as being "overheard" ("eloquence is heard, poetry is overheard"). When the narrator asks about Albertine, Marcel's love interest in *Remembrance of Things Past*, "Does / anyone really believe the / girl stays asleep for four / pages in volume V while / Marcel roams around her / prostrate form and / stretches out beside it on / the bed", we not only genuinely wonder alongside her, but are invited to hanker after the actuality behind the words. Together, we are looking through many screens, at multiple removes, but the effect is intimate. We are allowed into a private sphere of thought, as when the narrator of the first poem tells us that "reading [Proust] every day ... was like having an extra unconscious". At other times, however, we are left out in a way similar to an observation by Proust "G had underlined" with "red pencil":

[...] Proust
observes the momentarily
impaired surface of the
eye of a person who has
just had a thought she will
not tell you. It traces a
fissure in the pupil and
disappears back down its
own involuntary depths.
Watch the wake. (89)

We are limited to "the wake". Early in the book, M'hek tells Sad he has heard on the BBC that "*at the bottom of the ocean / is a layer of water that has / never moved*". This image could be a description of the unconscious, which also never moves, has no sense of time. However, we cannot dip in these waters. The "thought she will / not tell", the "involuntary depths", are dangled before us, but nonetheless we stay, along with the book's characters, on the surface.

Yet we stay by choice. There is the sense that a voyeuristic insistence into the depths would stir the waters, throw off the book's holding environment. Who amongst us wants to knock a child out of her mother's arms? Forcing someone to look at something is another kind of hold, one G calls "nakedness" – a nakedness he finds, sitting beside his dying mother's hospital bed, "*unforgivable*":

> And the
> reason he cannot bear her
> dying is not the loss of her
> (which is the future) but
> that dying puts the two of
> them (now) into this
> nakedness together that is
> *unforgivable*.

To not allow the book to set its own terms, set up its own system of defence, is to place the reader and writer in a similar, almost sado-masochistic, kind of hold, perhaps equally unforgivable.

In the end, although it is difficult to care much about the tedious characters and their labyrinths, they seem necessary to the writer's way of talking, which has – if the reader allows it, is willing to listen without memory, desire or understanding – the thrill of discovery, which is, perhaps, "the most part of happy". "Kindness," writes Adam Phillips, "is the ability to bear the vulnerability of others and therefore oneself." Vulnerability comes through even as the bulk of this writing serves as a distraction from, or container for, it. What the reader will do with that vulnerability is clearly a concern within the work, which may be why the book appears to be addressed to a reader who is willing to *bear* rather than *bare* it – to listen for the "zipper whine", hear the characters and their stories as necessary to these unzipped flashes, and resist any impulse to catch a glimpse of nakedness beneath.

Nuar Alsadir is the author of More Shadow Than Bird *(Salt, 2012).*

BRIGHT HARMONIES

Derek Mahon, Echo's Grove: Translations, *Gallery, €13.50*
ISBN 9781852355661

reviewed by Patrick Crotty

. . .

T he third book of *Metamorphoses* narrates in less than 50 lines the
tale of Echo, a mischievously articulate nymph condemned by an
enraged Juno to utter nothing for the rest of her life but the concluding
words of what her interlocutors say. Unable to express her love for
Narcissus, she loses her peace of mind and ultimately her body, dwindling
slowly to a voice that can be heard by everyone but can live only in the
loneliest of places. Derek Mahon's poem 'Echo' rearranges the syntax of
Ovid's account; by ending on the word "grove" it grants itself the status
of title poem to this rich and handsome collection of nearly 140 texts
based on originals drawn from across two-and-a-half millennia and from
four continents and a dozen languages.

Echo's Grove is an evocative, if in some respects startling, choice of title.
Echo, after all, has almost entirely lost her powers of articulation, and
hence the name of the book can be taken to imply that these
reformulations of the utterances of others are being offered in lieu of new
performances by a once commanding voice now reduced to mere mimicry.
It is true that decades have passed since the numinous lyrics of *Lives*

(1972), *The Snow Party* (1975) and *The Hunt by Night* (1982) gave Mahon a reputation as a poet of stylistic dash and philosophical daring beyond even the aspiration of most of his contemporaries. It is also true, however, that after a fallowish decade or so he has, since the mid 1990s, been publishing works which, for all their sometimes freewheeling and discursive character, have steadily increased in wattage up to *An Autumn Wind* (2010) and the more recent material in *New Collected Poems* (2011). While it seems unlikely that the poet is inviting us to think of the verses collected here as substitutes for some more real thing, he may be having a joke at his own expense, rather as he did in 1996 when he issued a selection of his criticism under the banner *Journalism*.

Looked at another way, the title *Echo's Grove* perhaps confers an unduly idyllic aura on the jungle of intertextuality through which a poet of any ambition has to hack a path. Mahon has always been frank about his sense of poetry as an echo-chamber, and his work has been unusually alert to the noises made by predecessors and contemporaries. His ironies have typically been a matter of recognising that other and more eloquent practitioners have already been in the sort of fix in which he finds himself. If the poetry has grown more allusive as it has relaxed into the colloquial tonalities of its later manner, it has from the beginning encompassed quotations from, and parodies of, the work of others, along with more or less straightforward translations. The latter have sometimes been absorbed into their new environments, as for instance in *The Yellow Book* (1997), where details in the versions of Juvenal and Baudelaire wittily reinforce the south Dublin setting of that work.

The significant fraction of the volume under review that has appeared in the author's individual collections – a particularly strong gust from *An Autumn Wind* blows through *Echo's Grove* – serves as a reminder of the longstanding intertextuality of Mahon's practice. The book is nevertheless to be recommended even to those with the individual volumes on their shelves, and not just because of the quality of the fresher material. Context is, if not all, at least hugely suggestive, and the arrangement of the poems in order of the births of their progenitors rather than on thematic grounds or by linguistic culture of origin facilitates the striking of bright new harmonies, for example through the juxtaposition of Chinese and Irish lyrics from the early medieval period or of French and Russian poems from the nineteenth century. If the organising principle recalls Robert Lowell's *Imitations* (1961), *Echo's Grove* displays a less persistent tendency than that still controversial compilation to make everything over in the image of its author. Only occasionally do we get a sense of an original desperately beating its wings against a pane of 'Mahonese', the default idiom of chatty, long-lined couplets with slant or otherwise muted rhyme with which we have been familiar since *The Hudson Letter* (1995): even though Narcissus never strays altogether far from the grove of Echo he cannot be said to have been allowed hog the show.

The extent to which Mahon endeavours to create direct anglophone analogues of originals from other languages varies greatly from poem to poem. Sometimes, indeed, the 'originals' exist only in his head, as in the case of the sequence of ecologically conscious poems attributed to an imaginary Indian contemporary called Gopal Singh and assembled under the teasing title 'Raw Material' at the end of the book. The piece Mahon allegedly makes out of Ibsen's *The Lady from the Sea* is almost equally 'original', a lyric dialogue based on the plot of the play rather than an attempted rendition of any sequence of words written by the Norwegian dramatist. In terms of verbal texture it owes far less to Ibsen than to 'The Great Silkie of Sule Skerry', the haunting Orcadian song of intercourse between seals and humans collected by Francis James Child as Ballad 113 and adapted by Mahon at two key junctures here. This brilliant and inventive variation on a theme bears only the most distant relation to translation as normally understood.

A look at the evolution of 'A Game of Cards', Mahon's 'take' on a Classical Irish *dán grá* (love poem) by Tadhg Ó Ruairc, provides an insight into how he makes his own of non-English materials. His first version, 'A Game of Cards and Dice' (2002), adhered to the detail of the late seventeenth-century text over 16 quatrains, faithfully reflecting its sexual drollery and offering a tantalising glimpse of aristocratic Gaelic mores in their twilight phase. Dropping seven stanzas along with the titular dice, and robustly reworking the remaining nine, 'A Game of Cards' displays little interest in the particulars of Gaelic historical experience and is concerned almost entirely – and entirely successfully – with recreating the erotic playfulness of the original in terms of the dandyish knowingness characteristic of Mahon's own poems. The result is a sprightly new English lyric that deserves to be cherished for its own sake but conveys almost nothing of the cultural otherness of the verses by Ó Ruairc that occasioned it.

Not all the texts mediated here have been so thoroughly appropriated, however, and it is difficult to generalise about the wide variety of effect on display across the volume. The angry, rasping 'The Same Ardour', a version from the French of the Haitian poet Jean-Fernand Brierre (1909-1992), sounds nothing like Mahon; along with a grave anti-slavery meditation by the Congolese Jean-Baptiste Tati Loutard (1938-2009), it made this reader shamefully aware of his ignorance of the anti-colonial literature of the Francophone world. The unmistakable electricity of poetry sizzles through the imitation of Jacques Prévert's well known 'Barbara' – another piece that wholly eschews the Mahonesque – and through the renditions of Sextus Propertius's 'Cynthia's Ghost', Ovid's 'Ariadne on Naxos', Laforgue's 'Travel Section', Rilke's 'Night Watch', Pasolini's 'Gramsci's Ashes' and a number of the lyrics by one of the poet-translator's living favourites, Philippe Jaccottet. Even to rehearse these names and titles is to suggest something of the scale of Mahon's engagement with the poetry of other ages and places. This vigorous and various book is likely to be seen as one cornerstone of his achievement.

Patrick Crotty edited The Penguin Book of Irish Poetry *(2010).*

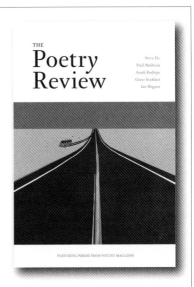

THE NATIONAL POETRY COMPETITION 2013

Judges: Julia Copus, Matthew Sweeney and Jane Yeh

The top three winners in the National Poetry Competition 2013 – Linda France, Paula Bohince and Josephine Abbott – were selected from a field of 12,000 poems from 70 countries. They are published for the first time, here in *Poetry Review*, and in an accompanying anthology, which also contains the poems by the seven commended poets. The judges share comments below on each of the winners.

Jane Yeh on Linda France's 'Bernard and Cerinthe'
This strange narrative of a man being seduced by a plant charmed us with its vivid imagery and linguistic wit. Its precisely honed couplets move from elegant description to a tragicomic climax, in which our hero finds himself "a buffoon in front of a saloon honey / high-kicking the can-can. Can't-can't". Truly imaginative and richly musical, 'Bernard and Cerinthe' is as much a pleasure on the page as it is on the tongue, and as such was the unanimous choice for first place.

Matthew Sweeney on Paula Bohince's 'Among Barmaids'
This taut, impressive poem constructs an extremely detailed picture of the rituals of the bar room. The voice of the poem, in the first person plural like a Greek chorus, delivers an incantation of great warmth in a cold place, brought home most vividly in the final image of the children brought to the bar by the men, to be spun on a make-believe dance floor by the ministering barmaids, trying to turn "despair into a party".

Julia Copus on Josephine Abbott's 'Love on a night like this'
This poem, built on motion, powerfully presents the balancing act of loving another human being. It depicts both the simplicity and enormity of that act, and our powerlessness in the face of it. We loved the atmosphere and detail – that plastic pot skittering on a path, birds "made helpless as plastic bags". This is a poem in which the personal and universal, the minute and the enormous, are made one and the same thing.

LINDA FRANCE

Bernard and Cerinthe

If a flower is always a velvet curtain
onto some peepshow he never opens,

it's a shock to find himself sheltering
from the storm in a greenhouse,

seduced by a leaf blushing blue
at the tips, begging to be stroked.

He's caught in the unfamiliar ruffle
of knickerbockers or petticoat, a scent

of terror, vanilla musk. If he were
not himself, he'd let his trembling lips

articulate the malleability of wax;
the bruise of bracts, petals, purple

shrimps; seeds plump as buttocks,
tucked out of harm's way, cocos-de-mer

washed up off Curieuse or Silhouette.
But being Bernard, he's dumbstruck,

a buffoon in front of a saloon honey
high-kicking the can-can. Can't-can't.

He attempts to cool himself, thinking
about sea horses, *Hippocampus erectus*,

listening to the rain refusing to stop,
soft against the steamed-up glass.

Linda France won first prize in the National Poetry Competition 2013.

PAULA BOHINCE

Among Barmaids

There was a metal door that took both hands
of a strong man to open

but we did it daily. Inside were our charges, sealed in
submarine darkness. We swam

through their booze, past the pool
table's alien island, darts that *thwacked* the pricked wall

like failure itself, spinning like downed ducks
to the filthy tile. Like good dogs, we fetched them.

In a windowless silence, we watched our drunks
bend like sycamores in an all-day snowstorm.

When they slept, we let them, then shook them
with the tenderness of mothers.

They woke and smoked, still dreaming, wore their trade
on their fingers – coal or dirt or grease.

On the jukebox, five songs repeated, each a lament
about cheating women. We hummed along,

bore the plodding joke, slurred compliment,
nodded at creased photographs of estranged children.

The beer rose in gushes. Our forearms bulged.
One girl, what she wanted before she died

was to see the ocean. Froth pillowed up
from subterranean barrels, through pipes and pulleys.

We wore out our pity, watching men stroke the bar
like the hardened brushed hair of a daughter.

We wore ours in scarves. Our hoop earrings swayed
on the downbeat. We held rags

or tucked them in jeans, tattooed the names
of ex-husbands, first lovers, into our skin

in script so thick and Bible-elaborate as to be illegible.
One wore her drugged-out son's childhood face

on her wrist, his doomed grin following us.
Men brought their kids when the wives needed peace.

We gave them Cokes and bowls of cherries,
let them draw on napkins and pinned up the drawings.

Sometimes we spun them on the make-believe dance
floor, trying to turn despair into a party.

Paula Bohince won second prize in the National Poetry Competition 2013.

JOSEPHINE ABBOTT

Love on a night like this

Outside, air is balancing itself. We can hear
branches in motion, some twigs breaking,

wires like violin strings, trees breathy as bass flutes.
The acoustics of friction. The science of equilibrium

isn't at all easy. Effort is needed
to walk against the wind. Love isn't easy.

Something – a plastic pot or a chair –
skitters on a path. A bin tips over.

Tonight, things are on the move:
leaves, dead and alive; seeds; fences;

flying insects and spiders new-worlded;
birds made helpless as plastic bags;

dust, sand, water, all turned to spray
and spread. Small trees blow over.

We are skittering on a path
though we're heavy with flesh, bone, eyes, tongues;

we're sea-birds in the teeth of a gale
trying to anchor ourselves in place;

we're storm-petrels, called little Peters because
we only look for a while as if we can walk on water;

Mother Carey's chickens;
oiseaux du diable.

Somewhere else, seas heap up and crests break.
Here, we're ditching meteorology for myth:

the wind's a creature broken out of a cave;
a wolf, and this is Ragnarök.

Glass breaks; a car alarm sounds; trees wrench.
There's a science and a logic to loving you,

but there's superstition on a night like this
and all the stirring of the world to settle first.

Josephine Abbott won third prize in the National Poetry Competition 2013.

Letter From Melbourne

OVERPLOTTED, DARL

Will Eaves

Angie's daughter, Stella, doesn't want to collect her order from Pizza Pizza. She doesn't want to go inside. She's 13, sensitive to the approach of adulthood and wary of adults for that reason. She has on her new white platform shoes and a short flared skirt. She saved up for the shoes – her first serious purchase. They cost $130, of which she had $100. Angie made up the difference. She sits outside the take-out restaurant. "It hasn't come," she says, when we drive to fetch her. "You have to ask, darling," Angie says, gently, "so they know you're here. How would they know otherwise?" Stella hugs her knees and looks to one side. "I don't like to."

I think I know how she feels. I wish I could tell her that being grown-up isn't anything to be scared of, but I can't. First of all, it's not a state you reach, it's an endlessly deferred prospect. Second, it is scary, because becoming anything means leaving behind something else, like childhood, just as – in my case – coming to Australia and announcing one's residency means leaving home and the UK.

Angie is the reason I first visited Melbourne, 15 years ago. She was getting married, I was working at the *TLS* and feeling fraudulent about my pretensions to write. I needed three clear weeks to push a first novel towards completion and I got them. The wedding was a joyous occasion, even for a gay gooseberry like me. I danced with her disreputable Auntie Marge and got sent off for foul play. On the same trip I met many new friends, went out into the Victorian bush, heard new and exotic birdcalls – the sonar-beep of the bell bird, the melodious argle-gargle of the Australian magpie – and sat out under the spilled Milky Way at night, enjoying the bounded freedom of the tourist who indulges a fantasy of self-recreation.

A lot has happened since then. The new and immediately familiar milestones click past: death of a parent, change of career, end of a relationship. I'm a sanguine person, it may surprise my friends to hear, and when Antony and I split up I decided there was nothing to stop me coming to Australia for a long stay. Melbourne has been good to me: I've written chunks of three books here. I canvassed opinion. Give it a go, was the broad consensus. I remember David Malouf saying he'd gone to Italy in the 70s to "see how he was" in another country and had come home ten years later with five or six novels, including *An Imaginary Life*, his best, a shamanic fantasia on Ovid in exile. So, for the first half of 2013, I busied myself administrating the move 10,000 miles south-east of SW2 and didn't stop to think about what the effects of moving – the disorientation, the dreamlike sense that the things one has done previously don't count and might actually have been unreal – would be like.

Because that's the substance of Ovid's story in the Malouf novella: distance is a journey in time, which makes everyone vanish. The immigrant is conspicuous, but feels invisible. You have your memories, for a while, but you're becoming someone new whether you like it or not, and those memories and psychological props, though sometimes sweet, are also out of place. To begin with, everything speaks of the past. Melbourne is a city of elms, those beautiful trees which in blossom look like a single elderflower and no longer exist in Britain. In Muscle Shoals, the record shop on Lygon Street, in the inner northern suburb where I now live, the proprietor plays 'Little Red Top' by King Pleasure, which my father used to sing along to. More profoundly, of course, the past speaks in the civic acknowledgements made during public concerts, readings and performances to the peoples who first lived here. Australians themselves exhibit a version of this what-has-been-lost vertigo, which goes along with a sense of being both the colonised and the conqueror.

But it's six months, roughly, since I relocated, and it's getting harder to ignore the signs that I am no longer merely elsewhere. Accepting a present shorn of the past can be chastening, like trying to ride a bike in the path-blocking squalls of a Melburnian winter (impossible), or coming across graffiti – "Hipster Scum Get Nothin' Done" – that suggests a reckoning is imminent. Mine came just a few weeks ago, on a walk to Merri Creek, which runs south into the Yarra and is a barometer of the changeable weather – now low, now full and roaring. There I sat down on a bench, on which someone had carved the words "You Are Here" and I realised, a bit late, that the answer to my mid-life jitters was just that.

In the car coming back from Pizza Pizza, Stella kicks off the white platforms and relaxes, hangs her legs over the back of Angie's driver's seat. The slice of pizza in her hands bends at the same angle as her calves. Angie, looking like she's wearing some sort of neckbrace or safety-harness, diagnoses my stuckness with the ease of a good reader. "You're overplotted, darl. Stop worrying about the outcome, get interested in the situation." I whine something about feeling I'm waiting, and Angie says, "Welcome to the party. Waiting is happening." And she's right. Easily the most devastating moment in the *Odyssey* is the encounter with Argos, Odysseus's faithful dog, who waits for ever for his master's return and then can't support the shock of getting what he wants: he dies, because the waiting is what mattered. Peter Porter's last poem, 'River Quatrains', is about waiting in bed for, well, the end, and even that vigil turns out to be alive with boat races, bars, chat, music. The whole point of suspense and comedy is that the set-up is what counts. Plots are pre-meditated and that's the problem: they don't allow for what *happens*. Aristotle says that there's a difference between "something happening after certain events and happening because of those events", i.e. narrative events should be consequential, but I'm not sure. Order tends to reveal itself, come what may. You think your diaries are orderless? Take another look at them. Most writers lie about the planning, anyway.

You write, you wait and see. That's how it goes. The coincidences that crop up, mysteriously, while you're waiting are proof that things are happening. Rhyme, in poetry, isn't so much about imposing a shape on language as showing how things in the real world chime with each other. Right now, for example, we're in Lorne, about two hours down the Great Ocean Road, and we can't get into town because there's some kind of fancy-dress swim carnival – from Angie's house on the hill I can just see a banana running up and down on the beach – and the place is gridlocked, so we have to wait. "Come and see the bowerbird", says Eddie, who is enthusiastically ten. He takes me into the garden, and over to a hide behind a laurel. Inside we can look out at a patch of shady forest-floor occupied by a shrine to waiting.

The bowerbird is a medium-sized passerine, with a unique claim to artistry. It is the only bird that builds an artifact, a work of art, other than its nest, to impress the ladies. The bower is a graceful passage-way construction, made out of thin but stiff grass and slender twigs, with tall sides, curved at the top like the lip of a lily. Around it in a sort of galactic disc is an explosion of bright blue odds and ends the bird has painstakingly collected – feathers, plastic straps, bottle-tops, glass fragments. It's a brilliant feat, to no certain end, because the female might not show. (She might get a better offer.) What's left is the situation, the thing the bird's amassed. "I am what is around me," said Wallace Stevens, nicely capturing the sense one has as a writer that to observe others is to be hidden oneself. "He's there," Eddie says, "but you can't see him."

When the bananas have crated themselves up and gone home, we go down to the beach and I buy a book by Stephen King (*On Writing*) in Fowlers, the excellent local second-hand bookshop. In this essay, King says that his stories are found objects that need careful extraction from their surroundings, like fossils. I don't know this at the time, of course; I read about it and write it up later – now, as it were – and I suppose I could be inventing the whole thing. But what is definitely happening is that Angie is organising an expedition to get food, because we ate most of Stella's pizza for her and she's still hungry and so are we. Eddie has an idea. He's a brave, experimental cook – some fungi had to be set aside yesterday – with a thing for weeds. He has a colourful book called *The Weed Forager's Handbook: A Guide to Edible and Medicinal Weeds in Australia*, and he wants to make Weedy Pasta. "Or pizza," says Stella.

We begin looking and the ingredients reveal themselves: plenty of prickly pear (a Mexican native) whose knobbly pads can be fried (the taste is tart but more-ish); wild brassicas (mustardy-hot cabbage), milk thistle and – almost everywhere – clumps of Fat Hen, which is a kind of spinach. All these plants are introductions of course, but Fat Hen comes with a story. Its Old English name is Melde, and until roughly the turn of the first millennium, the Derbyshire and Cambridgeshire family which eventually lent its name to the Australian city was spelled Melde-Bourne, because they grew the weed so prolifically in both counties. A weed you don't want, a crop you do. With a bit of patience you can sometimes turn one into the other.

Will Eaves has published one collection of poems, Sound Houses *(Carcanet, 2011). His latest book is* The Absent Therapist *(CB Editions, 2014), a volume of experimental fiction.*

CONTRIBUTORS

C.A. Conrad lives in Philadelphia. His books include *A Beautiful Marsupial Afternoon* (2012) and *The Book of Frank* (2010), both from Wave Books • **Greg Delanty**'s latest book is *The Greek Anthology, Book XVII* (Carcanet Oxford Poets, 2012). He teaches at St. Michael's College, Vermont • **Michael Dickman** was born in 1975 and is the author of two collections, *The End of the West* and *Flies*, both from Copper Canyon Press • **Steve Ely**'s first collection *Oswald's Book of Hours* (2013) is published by Smokestack Books • **Vicki Feaver**'s most recent collection is *The Book of Blood* (Cape, 2006) • **Adam Fitzgerald** was born in New York City in 1983. His debut collection *The Late Parade* (2013) is published by W.W. Norton • **Hannah Gamble** is the author of *Your Invitation to a Modest Breakfast* (2012), selected by Bernadette Mayer for the 2011 National Poetry Series • **Louise Glück** was born in 1943 in New York City. She won the Pulitzer Prize for *The Wild Iris* in 1992. She is a former US Poet Laureate and teaches at Yale University • **Meirion Jordan** has published two collections, *Moonrise* (Seren, 2008) and *Regeneration* (Seren, 2012) • **Martha Kapos**'s most recent collection is *Supreme Being* (Enitharmon, 2008). She is Assistant Poetry Editor of *Poetry London* • **Gregory Leadbetter**'s *Coleridge and the Daemonic Imagination* (Palgrave Macmillan) won the CCUE Book Prize 2012. His pamphlet *The Body in the Well* (HappenStance) appeared in 2007 • **Patricia Lockwood** is the author of *Balloon Pop Outlaw Black* (Octopus Books, 2012) and *Motherland Fatherland Homelandsexuals* (Penguin, 2014) • **Maitreyabandhu**'s first collection, *The Crumb Road* (Bloodaxe, 2013), is a PBS Recommendation • **Nate Marshall** is a poet and rapper from the South Side of Chicago. He is an MFA candidate in Poetry at the University of Michigan • **Ange Mlinko**'s most recent collection is *Marvelous Things Overheard* (Farrar, Straus and Giroux, 2013) • **Tomás Q. Morín**'s first collection is *A Larger Country* (2012), winner of *The American Poetry Review*/Honickman Prize • **Paul Muldoon**'s twelfth collection, *One Thousand Things Worth Knowing*, will be published in November by Faber • **Eileen Myles** was born in Cambridge, Massachusetts, in 1949. Recent books include *Sorry, Tree* (2007), *The Importance of Being Iceland: Travel Essays in ArtInferno: a poet's novel* (2010) • **Katrina Naomi** is completing a PhD in creative writing at Goldsmiths College • **Michael Robbins** is the author of *Alien vs. Predator* (Penguin, 2012) • **Simon Richey**'s first collection, *Naming the Tree*, will be published by Oversteps Books in April • **Amali Rodrigo** is a Sri Lankan writer currently based in Mumbai • **Martha Sprackland** was co-founder and Poetry Editor of *Cake* magazine. She is Assistant Poetry Editor at Faber • **Greta Stoddart** won the Geoffrey Faber Memorial Prize for *At Home in the Dark* (Anvil) in 2002. Her second collection is *Salvation Jane* (Anvil, 2008) • **Leah Umansky** lives in New York City. She is the author of the Mad-Men inspired chapbook *Don Dreams* and *I Dream* (Kattywompus Press, 2014), and the collection *Domestic Uncertainties* (BlazeVOX, 2013) • **Ocean Vuong** was born in Saigon and lives in New York City. He received a Pushcart Prize in 2013 • **Jan Wagner** was born in Hamburg in 1971. His collections include *Guerickes Sperling* (2004) and *Achtzehn Pasteten* (2007), both from Berlin Verlag • **Sarah Westcott**'s debut pamphlet *Inklings* was the PBS pamphlet choice for Winter 2013 • **Marcus Wicker** was born in Ann Arbor, Michigan. His first book is *Maybe the Saddest Thing* (Harper Perennial, 2012) • **John Hartley Williams**'s latest collection, *Assault on the Clouds*, was published by Shoestring in 2012.

poetryspace

**Annual International
Poetry Competition**

1st prize: £250
2nd prize: £100
3rd prize: £50

Judge: Alison Brackenbury
Closing date: June 30th 2014

www.poetryspace.co.uk

bodmin moor poetry festival

30 May - 2 June 2014

A fabulous, friendly poetry
festival in the heart of Cornwall's
beautiful Bodmin Moor

Talks, workshops, music,
theatre, film and visual art.
Highlights include National Poet
of Wales **Gillian Clarke**, **Louis
de Bernieres**, **Philip Gross**,
Menna Elfyn, **Rachael Allen**,
Alasdair Paterson, music
from **Jim Causley** and photos
by **Guy Gormley**

For more information
www.bodminmoorpoetryfestival.co.uk
davidwoolley.westwords@yahoo.com
Sterts Theatre & Arts Centre PL14 5AZ
01579 362382

Listen to...
THE
Poetry
Review

PODCAST RECORDINGS
with Colette Bryce, Sophie
Mayer, Jack Underwood,
Warshan Shire, Richard Scott
& Sam Willetts

PLUS INTERVIEWS & POEMS
by Matthew Dickman, Mark
Doty, Anne Gray & others

www.poetrysociety.org.uk

---

a place to write and be inspired

Loutro, Crete
June 2014

**June 03-10
'The American Poet'**
a poetry workshop with
**Kathryn Maris
& Maurice Riordan**

**June 10-17 & June 17-24
Poetry Retreats**
one-to-one guidance with
Mimi Khalvati

www.espirita.org.uk
espiritaorguk@aol.com
+ 44 (0)161 928 5768

LEDBURY POETRY FESTIVAL 2014

4-13 July 2014

Ten days of poetry, drama, film and music etc.
in the beautiful market town of Ledbury.

Ian McMillan, Sharon Olds, Robert Hass, Deryn Rees-Jones and artist Charlotte Hodes with a new commission inspired by the life of Helen Thomas, Robin Robertson, Motionhouse dance company, folk singer Alasdair Roberts with Hirta Songs, actress Juliet Stevenson performing Elizabeth Bishop, distinguished sound artist Chris Watson, Sujata Bhatt, Paul Henry, Kei Miller, The Poetry Trio with Wyn Hobson, The Hundred Years' War, Poetry and Meditation Retreat, The Elgar Chorale, actor Tom Durham performing Dauber by John Masefield, Michael Schmidt hosting 50 Shades of Gay, Owen Sheers on Dylan Thomas, Canadian poet and novelist Anne Michaels, Ledbury Liming, and much more.

Box office opens Monday 19 May 2014. 0845 4581743 poetry-festival.co.uk
INTERNATIONAL POETRY COMPETITION
Closing date 10 July 2014. Judge Ian McMillan. Adults, young people and children.
First Prize £1000. www.poetry-festival.co.uk/poetry-competition.html

 @ledburyfest

poetry-festival.co.uk

T.S. ELIOT INTERNATIONAL SUMMER SCHOOL
5-13 July 2014

The Institute of English Studies is hosting the sixth annual T.S. Eliot International Summer School. Poetry lovers and Eliot enthusiasts are invited to this week-long celebration of the life and writing of one of the greatest modern English poets. The summer school offers lectures and seminars, social evenings, excursions to Burnt Norton, Little Gidding and East Coker, and a poetry reading by Linda Gregerson, 2007 National Book Award Finalist.

For enquiries, registration and programme information:
http://ies.sas.ac.uk | Tel: +44 (0)20 7862 8679
E-mail: iesevents@sas.ac.uk | Twitter: @IES_London